Humanistic Anthropology

Humanistic Anthropology

Stan Wilk

The University of Tennessee Press
KNOXVILLE

To Rhona,
who has deepened my life beyond words,
and to our wondrous creations,
David and Joshua

Copyright © 1991 by The University of Tennessee Press / Knoxville.
All Rights Reserved. Manufactured in the United States of America.
First Edition

The paper in this book meets the minimum requirements of the
American National Standard for Permanence of Paper for Printed
Library Materials. ⊗ The binding materials have been chosen
for strength and durability.

The quotation from the *Tao Te Ching* by Lao Tzu, page 81, is from
the translation by D.C. Lau (Baltimore: Penguin, 1963). Reproduced by
permission of Penguin Books, Ltd.

Library of Congress Cataloging in Publication Data

Wilk, Stan.
 Humanistic anthropology / Stan Wilk. — 1st ed.
  p.   cm.
 Includes bibliographical references and index.
 ISBN 0-87049-679-4 (cloth: alk. paper)
  1. Philosophical anthropology. 2. Anthropology—Philosophy.
 3. Humanism. I. Title.
 BD450.W4979 1991
 128—dc20   90-39380   CIP

CONTENTS

PREFACE   vii

INTRODUCTION   ix

SECTION 1

1   Therapeutic Anthropology and
    Culture-Consciousness   3

2   Cultural Relativism and the Poetics
    of Self-Knowledge: The Story of Ruth   19

3   Biography and Natural Moral Being:
    The Teaching of Anthropology   35

SECTION 2

4   Magic, Science, and Religion   43

5   The Meaning of "Religion
    as a Cultural System"   67

6   Shamanism and the Cultural Thought
    of Edward Sapir   78

7   A Note on American Democracy
     and American Anthropology   93

     CONCLUSION

8   Humor and Culture:
     Anthropology and Human Consciousness   111

     REFERENCES   129

     INDEX   139

PREFACE

This book is the result of my effort to understand and then to communicate to my students the love I feel for anthropology. It has been an effort of some duration, and along the way I have been helped by a number of individuals and institutions. At Lycoming College I am indebted to John Whelan, David Rife, Owen Herring, and Richard Morris. The late Annemarie de Waal Malefijt instructed me in anthropology at Hunter College, and Arthur Tuden in the Graduate School of the University of Pittsburgh. I gladly acknowledge my debts and my gratitude to them both. I had the immense good fortune to attend a seminar on "Art and Society" sponsored by the National Endowment for the Humanities and presented by Philip Rieff, an incomparable teacher, and then another NEH seminar given by Jane Gary Harris, "The Poetics of Self-Knowledge: Russian Literary Autobiography in the Context of European Prose." I am indebted to both Rieff and Harris, and to the NEH. Miles Richardson, a source of personal inspiration, has been of great assistance, as has Roy Wagner. I would like to thank Lycoming College for its financial support through the years. This support has enabled me to devote time to my studies and to visit the American Philosophical Society and the Vassar College Library. The professional staffs of these two institutions have my gratitude. I thank the *Anthropology and Humanism Quarterly* for permission to use versions of "Therapeutic Anthropology and Culture- Consciousness" and "The Meaning of Religion as a Cultural System" which appeared in that fine journal. I wish to express my heartfelt appreciation to Dee Given who was kind enough to type the manuscript at Lycoming College and to the wonderful professional staff of The University of Tennessee Press, particularly Carol Wallace Orr, its director. Her encouragement was greatly appreciated. Special thanks also go to Mavis Bryant for a superb job of editing. Finally, I thank all those who have devoted their lives to the pursuit and dissemination of anthropological knowledge.

Anthropology is the science of the sense of humor. It can be thus defined without too much pretension or facetiousness. For to see ourselves as others see us is but the reverse and the counterpart of the gift to see others as they really are and as they want to be . . . Cannibalism shocks us terribly. Yet I remember talking to an old cannibal who, from missionary and administrator, had heard news of the Great War raging then in Europe. What he was most curious to know was how we Europeans managed to eat such enormous quantities of human flesh, as the casualities of a battle seemed to imply. When I told him indignantly that Europeans do not eat their slain foes, he looked at me with real horror and asked me what sort of barbarians we were to kill without any real object. In such incidents as these, the anthropologist learns to appreciate that Socratic wisdom can be best reached by sympathetic insight into the lives and viewpoints of others.

> Bronislaw Malinowski, Introduction to
> *The Savage Hits Back,* by Julius E. Lips

It is from the saving of expenditure in feeling that the hearer derives the humorous satisfaction.

> Sigmund Freud, *Character and Culture,*
> edited by Philip Rieff

INTRODUCTION

I

Scientific humanism is the moral practice of science, science itself
seen as culture, as expressive of a human way of life. Viewing humanistic anthropology as a process of personal sensemaking has led
me to see culture theory in terms of self and faith, in terms of natural
moral being.

The contemporary moral challenge, as I have come to understand it through humanistic anthropology, is the problem of "reading in." By "reading in," I mean our ability—indeed, our necessity—
symbolically to interpret our experience, to make it into meaningful
events. "Reading in" can be viewed naturalistically as the humanization of reality, the response of finite cultural creatures who need
an appropriately human sense of experience. Such a process can
only be addressed by personally embracing existential mystery.
From this perspective, the human paradox is located in meaningful or humane experience. Natural moral being begins with culture-
consciousness, with a deep acceptance of the natural truth that,
while we must shape experience to our nature, we must simultaneously shape our nature to human experience, historical, anthropological, and biographical.

Technology attempts to shape the material world to human de-
sires and calls this reason; scientific humanism attempts to shape the
human spirit to natural truth and calls this love. In this sense, scientific humanism is a neoshamanism, shamanism being a process of
personal sensemaking that antedates religion. As a humanist, I believe that it is reasonable to love.

I feel like the stereotypical comedian who asks, "Did you hear the
one about . . . ?" But rather than tell you about my wife, I shall tell
you about my mother as myself. Sometimes I look at my mother, who
is dying slowly in general but quite rapidly in mind, and I thank

nature for her obliviousness to her "medical" situation. To me she was a prehistoric cavewoman, an "earth-mother": proud, strong-willed, beautiful, good. She would put two fingers in her mouth and whistle down a New York City taxicab. She would open her second-floor apartment-house window and yell at two boys fighting in the street or three boys picking on a fourth. She loved to play gin rummy with her nephews for hours on end. I remember one time when I came home crying after being beaten up. She kicked me out the door and told me to fight my own battles. When I was driving her crazy, she would tell me that if I didn't stop, she would give me something to cry about. When relatives or friends were dying, they would ask for my mother if she was not already there. At least this is my childhood image of her.

Today, she sits in a wheelchair, oblivious to her son's particularity of kinship. I am, at most, a pleasant human presence; at least, not there at all. She urinates into a plastic bag and has lost control of much of her body. She seems oblivious to physical pain, for which I am grateful. My mother taught me "tough love."

It is not the physical indignities that pain me most; rather it is the hopefully irrational fear that she is still *in there*, aware of it all "on some level." For me, the worst part of watching my mother lose her mind is the strange realization that I hope she is no longer in her body. This is my sense of the "mind-body problem." Such a feeling, for it is that more than a thought, comes at the times I see tears in the corners of her eyes, merging and slowly rolling down her sallow, wrinkled cheeks. I think of the Joseph Cotton episode of "Alfred Hitchcock Presents" in which they almost buried Cotton alive before they noticed that he was crying in the coffin. When I see these tears I shiver with dread beyond my capacity to endure. The feeling enters my awareness like a hot potato I can only juggle until I drop it or pass it along to the vast realms of "out of mind," For if it were ever to enter my mind to stay . . . I must leave.

II
I have begun by offering a grace to words in an effort to describe the sensibility with which I speak as a Jewish-American anthropolo-

gist. In this section, I shall describe the studies I am offering in this book.

These essays explore the relationship between religion and science. Their focus is the newly emerging field of humanistic anthropology. In recent years, the American "Religious Right" has made a whipping-boy of their self-created straw person, "the secular humanist." This set of studies attempts to provide a humane understanding of their enemy.

The book is divided into four parts; a brief introduction and conclusion, a section on the nature of humanistic anthropology, and a section on that anthropology's relationship to supernatural beliefs.

The initial set of essays deals with the therapeutic implications of taking a naturalistic view of the human condition and understanding your own personal condition in that light. The first essay, "Therapeutic Anthropology and Culture-Consciousness," interprets Ruth Benedict's vision of humanistic anthropology as a therapeutic endeavor, by associating it with certain developments in cultural anthropology since her death in 1948, particularly the work of Clifford Geertz. By focusing on the interface of public and private life in the experience of Ruth Benedict and in my own, the second and third essays discuss the meaning to be discovered in the discipline of humanistic anthropology.

The second set of essays consists of studies in the anthropology of religion that seek to shed light on the relationship between science and religion by examining culture theory from the perspective of scientific humanism. The opening study, "Magic, Science, and Religion," presents an outline of one major historical stream of cultural thought on the relationship between natural and supernatural beliefs. The second essay, "The Meaning of Religion as a Cultural System," turns the tables on the "creation scientists" and offers anthropology as "religion." The third study, "Shamanism and the Cultural Thought of Edward Sapir," utilizes an appreciation of the original Don Juan tetralogy by Carlos Castaneda as a basis for exploring the humanistic aspects of symbolic anthropology in terms of personal meaning. The fourth and final essay in this section, "A Note on American Democracy and American Anthropology," addresses the separation of church and state from the perspective of scientific humanism. The concluding essay of the book, "Humor and Culture:

Edward Sapir's Concept of Culture," presents my understanding of culture by highlighting the unity of Edward Sapir's natural aesthetic of culture and Freud's therapeutic view of moral being, embodied in his brief note on joking.

SECTION I

Tradition is as neurotic as any patient; its overgrown fear of deviation from its fortuitous standards conforms to all the usual definitions of the psychopathic.

Ruth Benedict, *Patterns of Culture*

Contemporary theology reveals less about God than it does about the kind of men we are. It is largely an anthropological discipline. Today's theologian, be he Jewish or Christian, has more in common with the poet and the creative artist than with the metaphysician and physical scientist. He communicates a very private subjectivity. Its relevance lies in the possibility that he may enable other men to gain insight and clarify their religious lives in the face of a common experience.

Richard L. Rubenstein, *After Auschwitz*

Once upon a time, I, Chuang Chou, dreamt I was a butterfly, fluttering hither and thither, to all intents and purposes a butterfly. I was conscious only of my happiness as a butterfly, unaware that I was Chou. Soon I awaked, and there I was, veritably myself again. Now I do not know whether I was then a man dreaming I was a butterfly, or whether I am now a butterfly, dreaming I am a man.

Chuangtse, *The Wisdom of Lao Tzu*

1   *Therapeutic Anthropology*
   and Culture-Consciousness

The Contextual Background

Miles Richardson has written a moving personal discussion of anthropology, in which he states, "To me, anthropology was liberation" (1975:518). At the conclusion of his essay, Richardson asserts:

> The ability to symbolize makes us what we are. It accounts for our successes; it is the reason for our failures. Being a human is an impossible task . . . The anthropologist's job is to tell of that task, to glorify man by composing and reciting with skill and passion the human myth . . . As teller of the human story, the anthropologist cannot falsify what we are. He seeks to find the full range of human variation, the cruelty, the magnificence, the love that is in us all and in all of our cultures. But the anthropologist is not a passive recorder of human data; he searches for the human secret . . . In telling the human myth, of how men wrestle with the problem of being human, of how a people envision a society of love but live in a society of hate, of how they conceive of a collective soul but live in individual cells, the anthropologist may find his own salvation. (1975:530)

To me, anthropology is a world I inhabit. It is my essential cultural reality, to which I adapt and through which I define my existence. Moreover, I trust and believe that I am not alone in my experience of the world of anthropology. It is to you, my fellow inhabitants of this world, that I address these thoughts, in the hope that I will hear and learn more about them from you. Bob Scholte (1969) called for increasing development of a reflexive anthropology. To me, such a call constitutes a plea for increased awareness of one's existence — for greater self-consciousness, greater consciousness of reality. Such goals are fundamental to the calling and discipline of anthropology.

They constitute the continually receding destination point whose pursuit can enliven a culture that is truly our profession. It is my contention that such a reflexive anthropology offers great opportunities for the development of therapeutic anthropological traditions within the culture of anthropology itself. Reflexive anthropology can accomplish this in part by prompting us to ask neglected questions that can serve as a foundation for expanding the personal dimensions of anthropology. How does the culture of anthropology affect anthropologists as human beings? Analytically speaking, what is the cultural reality we enter as anthropologists? The study of the impact of anthropology on our own existence is a fundamental dimension of both reflexive and therapeutic anthropologies.

The approach that I take is implicitly relational and thereby processual in nature. A. Irving Hallowell (1967) stressed the relationship between self-image, experience and its interpretation, and social order and ordering. By focusing primarily on Ruth Benedict's classic *Patterns of Culture*, this essay will explore one component of a processual dynamic in the hope of sketching a therapeutic anthropology that can emerge from the consideration of self as mystery. In essence, the examination of self and other continues to be an intimate part of a dynamic anthropological process. The experiential unity of this process can still enliven and move those who seek it out. Potentially, the process can mediate the discontinuities of categorical distinction — the discontinuities of the social and the psychological, of the personal and the political.

I see the development of therapeutic anthropologies as a movement committed to the use of anthropological materials in the service of mythic creation. I see modern myth as a movement beyond, rather than in opposition to, the existent facts. Existent facts certainly should not be ignored or undervalued, but therapeutic anthropologies as humanistic endeavors must explore fully the realm of human possibility (see Wilk 1976). It is not the separation of myth from concrete event — to my mind, an impossibility — that is my ultimate goal (see Harris 1968:448), but rather the mastery of the mythic medium so as to promote concrete events that are enriching in human terms, and minimize degrading ones.

As I have stated elsewhere, "all interpretation is consciously descriptive, and all description, verbal or otherwise, is symbolic" (Wilk 1977).

In Hallowell's terms, therapeutic anthropologies will concentrate on "the symbolic transformation of experience" (1967:8; see also Langer 1957). Ernst Cassirer, a leading student of mythology, was so appalled by political life in this century, particularly the rise of Nazi Germany, that he choose to stress only the negative dimensions of mythology. By presenting this negative assessment as the whole truth, he sought to contribute to the banishment of the mythic dimension from human life. While I deeply appreciate his concerns, I cannot agree that the solution to the very real dangers lies in banishing mythology. I simply do not believe that we have this choice, but even if we could, we should not choose to do so. Rather we should cultivate a full awareness of the role of the mythic in human dynamics. We must be prepared to accept responsibility, to embrace the implications, of the process we consciously seek to influence. With this contextual background in mind, I wish to embark on a very limited exploration of the anthropological tradition, from the perspective of "models for."

The Self and Culturally Molded Experience

The following discussion is based on the assumption that a therapeutic anthropology can emerge by focusing on culturally molded experience. As Ruth Benedict has noted:

> The vast proportion of all individuals who are born into any society always and whatever the idiosyncrasies of its institutions, assume . . . the behavior dictated by that society. This fact is always interpreted by the carriers of that culture as being due to the fact that their particular institutions reflect an ultimate and universal sanity. The actual reason is quite different. Most people are shaped to the form of their culture because of the enormous malleability of their original endowment. They are plastic to the molding force of the society into which they are born . . . the great mass of individuals take quite readily the form that is presented to them. (1959:254–55)

While Benedict's remarks on "ultimate and universal sanity" are of continuing importance, and while her wonder at the profound variability of human experience continues to be a wellspring of humanistic anthropology, we are only beginning to appreciate the implications of her study of the human condition for our understanding of human consciousness. Anthropologists have been busy defending their discipline's right to exist, by emphasizing one side of a relationship, one element in a transaction—the cultural influence on human experience. With Leslie White, they have dwelt too long on a culturology that sees human behavior as a dependent variable: "A people's behavior is a response to, a function of, their culture. The culture is the independent, the behavior the dependent, variable; as the culture varies so will the behavior. . . . The scientific explanation does not take the people into account at all" (1959:241–42). Through the conscious development of concepts such as cultural realities, we can begin to explore the human influence on cultural experience. By *cultural realities*, I mean the various worlds we live in as human beings, subjective realities personally experienced and in large part symbolically constructed. Such realities may include, but are not limited to, what is recorded by machines or postulated by "objective science" as independent external reality. For my purposes, cultural realities are more fully the human worlds containing reasons, value, meaning, motivation, and feeling—in short, human experience. In cultural realities, duration is not limited to clock time but rather centers on the human experiences of the passing one's life. Time can pass slowly, as when one anxiously waits in stormy weather for the anticipated arrival of a loved one, or quickly, as when one witnesses a young child's first experience of a warm, majestic ocean. For the most part, cultural realities contain components which are symbolically mediated rather than simply recorded in human awareness. The earth, as contained in cultural realities, is fundamentally the human environment. It is not limited necessarily or exclusively to the earth of geology, botany, and zoology, but also contains the manifold potentiality inherent in symbolic mediation. It may be the Bambuti's (Turnbull 1962) "gift of the forest spirit" or the modern businessman's "commodity" (Polanyi 1944). My primary concern in these remarks is not with the ontological status of cultural realities, real though they be, but with their human consequences. For while it is true, as Benedict notes, that "the great mass of individuals take quite readily the form that is presented to them," it is my contention that there are serious problems with our cultural form which warrant careful investigation. I believe these problems are of such dimensions that one can question our very possession of culture in its deepest and highest manifestations. Moreover, I believe that Ruth Benedict, among others, has provided a key to unlock the passage to a more satisfying modern existence. That key lies in the realization that culture and individual human beings are simply two conceptual points of departure, two perspectives and entries onto a dynamic process, the process of human experience.

Human experience is here assumed to be a self-construction as well as an imposition. The field in which this process unfolds can be termed human consciousness. If it has any potential, human consciousness above all else is capable of bringing into being subjective realities, cultural realities. For the purposes of this presentation, all other supposed states of this field (whether termed the unconscious, objective consciousness, etc.) will be taken as manifestations of faith called forth by the symbolics of myth. *Myth* is a term here used to denote the verbal symbolic that is made humanly compelling by personal and broader social context. *Faith* is here used to denote the existential experience of being compelled. There can be no faith without myth, and no vital myth without faith.

Symbolic anthropology makes clear that symbol and human experience are intimately related. Conceiving of cultures as symbol systems allows us to gain greater precision in our attempts to understand the imposition of cultural realities. As with Benedict's work, however, we are only beginning to appreciate the self-contained nature of the process: symbol to experience, experience to symbol. Clifford Geertz is guided by the realization that cultural systems are models of and for experience. He states that "culture patterns have an intrinsic double aspect: they give meaning, i.e., objective conceptual form, to social psychological reality, both by shaping themselves to it and by shaping it to themselves" (1973:93). He is cognizant of the fact that models of and for reality are to a significant degree interchangeable or, as he phrases it, "inter-transposable": "The inter-transposability of models for and models of, which symbolic formulation makes possible, is the distinctive characteristic of our mentality" (1973:93). The causal arrow of culture theory is beginning slowly to turn back upon itself, as the circularity of the process is appreciated more fully. Margaret Mead said of Ruth Benedict:

I believe *Patterns of Culture* has lived because of her robust conviction that a knowledge of how culture works gives to human beings a greater control over their own future than they have ever known before. It comes as a surprise to the reader, first caught in a recognition of the strength of the cultural web, to have this very strength in the end turned back into the context of a mankind, grown wise through knowledge of the very cultural web in which he first appeared to be caught. (1959b:x)

The primary consequence of this realization for the development of therapeutic anthropologies is a conceptualization of the life-worlds of human experience as dynamic reciprocal processes, as arenas for the interplay of relative causations and effects. Concepts will be utilized so as to highlight interdependence in the context of a dynamic, holistic orientation. From such a grounding, even "common sense" is rendered extraordinary. And from this grounding we can appreciate the compatibility of Geertz's realization with that of Theodore Roszak, who stresses the intimate dialectic between the questions "How shall we know?" and "How shall we live?" (1969:233). At the very least, our descriptions of experience can significantly influence and shape future manifestations of that experience; at most, they can determine the very nature of these manifestations. As Geertz has noted, the comparative investigation of common sense should contribute to the movement "away from functionalist accounts of the devices on which societies rest toward interpretive ones of the kinds of lives societies support" (1975:26). The journey from models *of* to models *for*, and back — the realization of culture process or what Ruth Benedict termed "culture-consciousness"— is, I believe, fundamentally transformative, and of lasting human worth.

In the field of human consciousness, awareness is the medium of experience, and heightened awareness a medium of analysis and transformation. A. Irving Hallowell realized that heightened self-awareness in human beings is the necessary prerequisite for cultural life, over and above the purely instinctual (Hallowell 1967). The sense of self, with its attendant sense of personal responsibility, is necessary in order to create the moral creature in the image of the moral order. This increase in awareness allowed proto-humans to enter into human cultural existences, to become dream animals. As Loren Eisley wrote so beautifully of *homo sapien*:

He was becoming something the world had never seen before — a dream animal — living at least partially within a secret universe in his head with other, similar heads. Symbolic communication had begun. Man had escaped out of the eternal present of the animal world into a knowledge of past and future. The unseen gods, the powers behind the world of phenomenal appearance, began to stalk through his dreams. (1946:120)

Human beings, however, only recently have begun the study of the secret universes of cultural realities, and even more recent is the realization of the human creative contribution to these universes.

It is not surprising that these developments occur in relation to a fundamental transformation of culture, which anthropologists generally conceptualize as the movement from primitive to civilized. Others have viewed this transformation as fundamentally a movement from dream to nightmare. Our present awakening from the nightmare, with its attendant possibility of coming to culture-consciousness, is, I believe, potentially as profound a development in human history as was the coming to self-consciousness. Indeed, this new state may alter our self-consciousness significantly. The possibility of profound transformation in the quality of human experience, in the quality of human cultural realities, is opened up by our intensified awareness of the dreamer and the dreamed. Both the materialism of our present lives and the emphasis on the therapeutic reflect the potentiality of transformation. While it is personally difficult to say, and more difficult to do, we must overcome our fear of dreaming anew. But just as we must lie in our own beds, so we had better dream our own dreams.

How else but as the awakening from a nightmare are we to understand the following analysis of the human career offered up by Jules Henry in *Culture Against Man*?

If this book can be said to have a message, it is that man wrings from culture what emotional satisfactions he obtains from it. But this is part of the evolutionary process. Man shall not wait 200 million years, like the giant tortoise within his carapace, until some organized mutation determines his course; rather shall he hunt, in anguish and perplexity, for a pattern of decent relations with his fellows. For man is deprived of inborn ways to interpersonal satisfaction and thus is compelled to search for them, evolving along the resulting pathways of dissatisfaction and intrapsychic conflict . . . in this strain toward decency man is heir to a primitive condition which continues to confuse his social and personal life. Throughout history, in jungle and coral atolls, and stone pavements inhabited by men, society has been established primarily for the purpose of guaranteeing food and protection. And from this primitive necessity has emerged the central problem of the human species: the fact that inner needs have scarcely been considered . . . everywhere man has literally had to force from an otherwise efficient society the gratification of many of his inner needs. The one-side emphasis on survival, however, has provided man with an evolutionary impulse, for in the effort to gratify himself emotionally and to rid himself of emotional conflict with himself and his fellows, man constantly works on his institutions and on himself and thus becomes self-changing. Meanwhile, the orientation of man toward survival, to the exclusion of other considerations, has made society a grim place to live in, and for the most part human society has been a place where, though man has survived physically he has died emotionally. (1963:11–12)

This awakening, as of a child in the darkness of the night, calls forth a need for comforting rather than comfort, for therapy; and so cultural analysis, symbolic analysis, becomes a therapeutic endeavor. Culture itself enters our heightened awareness as a therapeutic system. The symbolic analysis by Clifford Geertz clearly displays this therapeutic emphasis, as do, even more unabashedly, the writings of Philip Rieff, who maintains that it "is to control their dis-ease as individuals that men have acted culturally, in good faith" (1966:3). Rieff sees each culture as "its own order of therapy—a system of moralizing demands, including remissions that ease the pressures of communal purposes" (1966:15). He notes that "all symbol systems are therapeutic if they are compelling enough, and especially so if they serve to introduce a character ideal" (1966:66). This reading of culture is a logical complement to Loren Eisley's reading of human evolution, as emergence of human consciousness—the emergence of the patient.

> The story of Eden is a greater allegory than man has ever guessed. For it was truly man who, walking memoryless through bars of sunlight and shade in the morning of the world, sat down and passed a wondering hand across his heavy forehead. Time and darkness, knowledge of good and evil, have walked with him ever since. It is the destiny struck by the clock in the body in that brief space between the beginning of the first ice and that of the second. In just that interval a new world of terror and loneliness appears to have been created in the soul of man. (Eisley 1946:125)

While the new heightened awareness of culture can transform and enrich human experience in a manner that is in keeping with the effect of all increases in awareness, it can also increase our responsibility. As Robert Redfield has written: "I cannot prove to you that man should act more decently and more humanely. I follow Kroeber in saying that on the whole he has come to. When, now, he does not, it is a worse mistake than when he did not in precivilized times. We have come to know better, however better is to be justified philosophically" (1953:164). Our new responsibility to self and others is not simply to conform, fit in, perpetuate or survive, but, as Benedict was well aware, to create. Toward the end of *Patterns of Culture*, she notes, "No society has yet attempted a self-conscious direction of the process by which its new normalities are created in the next generation" (1959:271). She had previously stated that "there is . . . one difficult exercise to which we may accustom ourselves as we become increasingly culture-conscious. We may train ourselves to pass judgment upon the dominant traits of our own civilization" (1959:249). But here we confront a critical modern dilemma—we must assume responsibility just when our traditional cultural comfortings are least satisfying and/or effective. It would appear that Durkheim's relationship to religion is modern humanity's relationship to culture-consciousness in general. As Evans-Pritchard observed: "If Durkheim's theory of religion is true, obviously no one is going to accept religious beliefs any more, and yet on his own showing, they are generated by the action of social life itself, and are necessary for its persistence" (1965:64–65). That Durkheim's dilemma should be the modern dilemma is not surprising, for it was fundamentally a result of the process of deculturation through heightened cognitive awareness. It is to this dilemma that I wish to turn, for I believe it is a central concern for any developing therapeutic anthropology.

To begin with, if we are in such a dilemma, we should acknowledge it, for failure to do so eliminates the only sense in which we have any real choice, the choice of assuming responsibility (Castaneda 1971:164). Philip Rieff has written the following:

> Undeceived, as they think, about the sources of all morally binding address, the psychologizers, now fully established as the pacesetters of culture change, propose to help men avoid doing further damage to themselves

12 *Humanistic Anthropology*

by preventing live deceptions from succeeding the dead ones. But, in order to save themselves from falling apart with their culture, men must engender another, different and yet powerful enough in its reorganization of experience to make themselves capable again of controlling the infinite variety of panic and emptiness to which they are disposed. (1966:3)

It is my belief that anthropologists—as experts on myth and ritual, belief and behavior, culture process; as cultivators of culture-consciousness, of mediums of meaning—will play an increasing role in this process. In considering how we should go about this task, on behalf of ourselves and others, in the context of the modern dilemma I have indicated, we can gain direction from several observations by Thomas Szasz in his book *Heresies*: "It is impossible to forget something by dint of effort. Memories, good or bad, cannot be removed as if they were art objects or pieces of junk . . . the way to achieve superior skill in forgetting (what one wants to forget) is not by practicing the art of forgetting (since there is no such art), but by practicing the art of learning" (1976:172).

Certainly learning the art of culture-consciousness through learning the art of learning, a significant dimension of culture process, is a glowing bubble, one which beckons us to burst in onto a world of possibility. That world of possibility is, in significant dimensions, the world of "eternal return" (Eliade 1971):

Primitives treat objects as agents; we call these people "savages" and their outlook on life "animism." Psychiatrists treat agents as objects; we call these people scientists and their outlook on life "humanism."

The primitive tries to understand nature in terms of human nature. The psychiatrist tries to understand human nature in terms of nature. Scientists have corrected the savage's mistake. Who will correct the psychiatrist's? (Szasz 1976:175)

It is with pleasure and excitement that we collectively reply to Szasz's rhetorical question with the basic commitment of the anthropological tradition: the primitive shall correct us! I, like many whom I trust, was first drawn to anthropology by the promise of wisdom to be learned from the many forms of cultural existence that is our subject matter. As Elinore Smith Bowen (1964:283–97) so honestly illustrates, the recognition of our own ignorance is the first step toward discovery and appreciation of the wisdom that is all around us:

In natural science, the task is to make new discoveries and to formulate novel theories, and to have the courage of propounding them in opposition to established knowledge. In moral science, it is to rediscover old observations and to rearticulate ancient principles and to have the courage to defend them in opposition to the pretensions of scientism. (Szasz 1976:177)

I take from this that we should not expect to find new answers as much as come to appreciate old truths in our investigation of culture-consciousness. Humanistic anthropology in general will largely be a process of recovery . . . a therapeutic endeavor.

Let us turn our attention directly upon culture-consciousness. A basic and substantial portion of anthropology is predicated upon the assumptions that culturally induced experience is human experience, and that a substantial portion of human experience is culturally induced experience. The nature of culturally induced experience, which is just the metaculture of naturally induced cultural experience, is a matter of primary importance for our appreciation of culture-consciousness. Knud Rasmussen relates the following remarks of Orulo, wife of the shaman Aua. He had been questioning Orulo about some of the inconsistencies in a myth she had related to him. This had only led to their mutual confusion. Rasmussen relates that finally Orulo laughed and said,

> Too much thought only leads to trouble. All this that we are talking about now happened in a time so far back that there was no time at all. We Eskimos do not concern ourselves with solving all riddles. We repeat the old stories in the way they were told to us and with the words we ourselves remember. And if there should then seem to be a lack of reason in the story as a whole, there is yet enough remaining in the way of incomprehensible happenings, which our thought cannot grasp. If it were but everyday ordinary things, there would be nothing to believe in. How came all the living creatures on earth from the beginning? Can anyone explain that?

And then, after having thought for a moment, she added the following, which shows in a striking fashion how little the actual logical sequence counts with the Eskimos in their mythology:

> You talk about the stormy petrel catching seals before there were any seals. But even if we managed to settle this point so that all worked out as it

should, there would still be more than enough remaining which we cannot explain. Can you tell me where the mother of the caribou got her breeches from; breeches made of caribou skin before she had made any caribou? You always want these supernatural things to make sense, but we do not bother about that. We are content not to understand. (1930:69)

In our efforts to help humanity survive and flourish, I believe we have much to learn from Orulo concerning the art of living, concerning the art of appreciating and adjusting to the universals of the human condition. Specifically I wish to explore the possibility that no full and final answer will ever come to the question of the nature of culture process, that mystery is and will remain the bedrock, the grounding of human existence. Whether the mystery of experience is expressed in terms of arbitrariness, circularity, unknowability, possibility, creativity, irreducibility, or whatever, is not important for the moment; they are all forms of mystery.

I believe that it was from this realization that Siegfried Nadel analyzed the processes of conformity and, ultimately, of sociocultural existence. He concluded his analysis with the following statements on the essential and irreducible datum of cultural existence, "values simply held":

We have in the last resort, merely multiple instances of a given system of values, irreducible to any further regulative machinery save that circular process mentioned before (values engender conduct and conduct reinforces values) which seems inherent in any value system of real efficacy . . . the specific controls are equally fitted into the circularity of value systems. For the controls both follow from the value system and demonstrate it. (1953:272–73)

Whenever I reread these words, I stand back and marvel with Nadel at his realization, some of the implication of which I am considering indirectly in this essay. Culturally molded experience as mystery: this is to my mind true. I am captivated and fascinated by the vistas opened up by the conscious cultivation of this realization. I believe that it is a key to an appreciation of culture-consciousness and that a therapeutic anthropology can emerge from the anthropological consideration of cultural realities, symbolic realities, as existential mystery.

A therapeutic anthropology grounded in human experience as existential mystery will be rooted in the field of human consciousness and in an appreciation of human being as symbolic being. To see human being as symbolic being points toward other things: the social other and the creation of collective meaning, cultural existence as a shared stance toward life. Symbolic existence that does not partake in cultural existence in this sense will be problematic in critical respects and inherently unstable. Human beings, as symbolically conscious creatures, have symbolic needs that must be satisfied by culture process. These needs will either be satisfied or provide the source of energy for much of human social dynamics, precipitating, among other things, the symbolics of therapy. Jules Henry (1963) understood this well, understood this fundamental source of dynamism in human behavior and in much of what we now call social change. Anthony Wallace (1956), through his conceptualization of revitalization movements; Siegfried Nadel (1953), through his cybernetic conceptualization of human social life; and Francis Hsu (1971), through his conceptualization of psychosocial homeostasis, displayed similar understandings.

As Leslie White stressed, human existence is cultural existence, and cultural existence is based on the ability to symbolize. For many years, however, White did not fully appreciate the problematics involved in the cultural or symbolic foundation of human existence. For human beings exist in life-worlds capable of manifesting purpose and meaning which cannot simply be imposed from without, but which rather must be made manifest, experienced, acknowledged, and held, from within. We are only beginning to appreciate the dimensions of these problematics. The perspective in traditional culture-and-personality studies has emphasized the cultural imprint on human potentiality, reflecting a pronounced tendency to pursue the development of a generalizing science. But to even *that* goal, there is more than one path. To see meaning as imposed is in serious respects to oversimplify. An emphasis on the mutuality of sociality that is involved in the most potent creation of meaning, its collective creation, is a necessary corrective. As White (1959:243–46) stressed, "strictly speaking, the symbolic conceptualization of culture does not depend on its collective nature aside from the fundamental sociality of human existence" (244). However, the human consequences of culture, its therapeutic consequences, certainly are affected in significant ways by the collective dimension of its existence. By focusing on the problematics of meaningful human existence, we can explore a greater variety of analytical emphases. In this essay, for instance, I am suggesting a perspective on culture as a mutual, experientially based creation of human consciousness. The study of culture, as such, offers a richer opportunity to appreciate the less obvious needs and demands inherent in the human condition, and their consequences. However, while the collective must continue to be important, we must not slight the individual and idiosyncratic. Indeed, we must seek more fully to appreciate the interaction and blending of the collective and individual, as, for example, in the American Indian vision quest. But most importantly, we must fully explore how culture manifests human consciousness and how, in fundamental ways, human consciousness and cultural creations can develop disharmonies.

It is, I believe, from a sense of disharmony that culture-consciousness can emerge. This is true whether the disharmony is that seen by Henry (1963) as "culture against man," by Redfield (1953) as a decline in the dominance of the moral order, by Hsu (1971) as a lack of psychosocial homeostasis, by Sapir (1924) as spurious culture, by Mary Ellen Goodmen (1967) in the need for autonomy, or by Benedict (1959) as a lack of integration or a low ranking in the scale of human values. The nightmare has not been in vain, for from the suffering a new awakening can emerge, a deepened appreciation, a therapeutic appreciation, of the human cultural condition. This appreciation — whether expressed in the shamanic metaphor of death and rebirth; or in the dynamics of despair and hope, of alienation, transcendence, and immersion; or in deculturalization and reculturalization — is the realization of human existence as process. Cultural existence is an ongoing process in which disillusionment is the necessary prerequisite for the emergence of the newly saving illusion. To see the end of a partial perspective is the opportunity to realize more fully the dynamic whole, of which that part is but a finite and hence partial manifestation, so that when inevitably we enter anew into a partiality we do so with a fuller appreciation of its finite and arbitrary nature. Hopefully we can see the edge as a border, the end as a new beginning, and thus recapture the primitive sense of cycle and eternal return.

In a sense, the myth I am seeking to enliven seeks to counter the myths of opposition; the opposition of the individual and the social, of the mystic and the scientist, of the instinctual and the willed, of the natural and the cultural. The myths of opposition are finite and thus limited perspectives on a processual harmony to which we must surrender by embracing and exhibiting. If we can symbolically embrace the oppositions; acknowledge the ambivalences, the absence of a sense of wellbeing; and claim them for our very selves, we are well on our way to exhibiting a therapeutic anthropology.

The dynamics of awareness, fear, and trust are at the roots of anthropology as much as they are at the roots of the shamanic discipline. Embracing the mystery of experience and thus the mystery of the self is as fundamental to the attainment of culture-consciousness, to its realization rather than simply its acknowledgment, as it is to the attainment of shamanic status and the successful conclusion of a variety of other symbolic apprenticeships that fruitfully can be viewed from the perspective of the therapeutic. We are, after all, little changed from the Jívaro youth who must have the courage to move forward and encounter the horrific vision so as to bring about its transformation into his life-giving soul (Harner 1967:182).

Prior to her entrance into the discipline of anthropology, Ruth Benedict wrote the following lines in her journal regarding her requirements for an essential sense of wellbeing:

> to find a way of living not utterly incongruous with certain passionate ideals: to attain to a zest for life, an enthusiasm for the adventure which will forever deliver me from my shame of cowardice, to master an attitude toward life which will somehow bind together these episodes of experience into something that may conceivably be called life. (Quoted in Mead 1974:10)

It is my faith that she found what she was searching for in the attainment of culture-consciousness, which comes from, leads to, and radiates tolerance. It is from a responsible tolerance of self and other that a humanistic and compassionate therapeutic anthropology can fully emerge, for tolerance is the gateway to appreciation. Such tolerance is not simply a cognitive position or possession; it is, even more, an experiential realization. The shaman Don Juan has said: "The art of a warrior is to balance the terror of being a man with the wonder of being a man" (Castaneda 1972:315). The tolerance I speak of is the balancing of the wonder of empathy with the terror of responsibility. As with all balancing acts, the risk of a fall is ever-present. Thus it is important that we not look down, but rather keep our heads straight so as to see our destination. As Ruth Benedict envisions in the closing line of *Patterns of Culture*; "We shall arrive then at a more realistic social faith, accepting as grounds of hope and as new bases for tolerance the coexisting and equally valid patterns of life which mankind has created for itself from the raw material of existence" (1959:278).

2 Cultural Relativism and the Poetics of Self-Knowledge: The Story of Ruth

Hath not a Jew eyes? hath not a Jew hands, organs, dimensions, senses, affections, passions? fed with the same food, hurt with the same weapons, subject to the same diseases, healed by the same means, warmed and cooled by the same winter and summer, as a Christian is? If you prick us, do we not bleed? if you tickle us, do we not laugh? if you poison us, do we not die? and if you wrong us, shall we not revenge?

William Shakespeare, *The Merchant of Venice*

One can learn of the mystery of consciousness by contemplating the instant before one thinks and realizing the degree to which one has no control over the matter yet the utmost conviction that one will be capable of doing it. The mystery of consciousness is the personal realization of the necessity of faith.

Ruth Benedict looked at human life in affective terms, as a feeling consciousness. She brought a poet's vision to anthropology. As Shelley has written:

The most unfailing herald, companion, and follower of the awakening of a great people to work a beneficial change in opinion or institution is poetry. At such periods there is an accumulation of the power of communicating and receiving intense and impassioned conceptions respecting man and nature. The person in whom this power resides, may often as far as regards many portions of their nature, have little apparent correspondence with that spirit of good of which they are the ministers. But even whilst they deny and abjure, they are yet compelled to serve, the Power which is seated upon the throne of their own soul. (1965:79)

In this essay I shall examine some of the poetic elements in Ruth Benedict's masterwork of humanistic anthropology, *Patterns of Culture*, for the light they shed on the doctrine of cultural relativism. For I believe that today is a time of awakening, and I believe that one can awaken to anthropology only by understanding the poetry of cultural relativism as Ruth Benedict did—as the universal logic of human emotions.

I believe Ruth Benedict came to anthropology in search of a vision. The vision she found is that of a world experienced from culture-consciousness, the world of common humanity seen from the perspective of cultural relativism. Looking in retrospect at her work—from her doctoral dissertation, *"The Concept of the Guardian Spirit in North America,"* through her last major book, *The Chrysanthemum and the Sword: Patterns of Japanese Culture*—one can see a journey, a search for a guiding vision. That vision she was destined to discover in cultural relativism and express artfully in her mature thought. In *Patterns of Culture*, she talks about ways of "arriving at the value of existence" (1959:78). The doctrine of cultural relativism was her way. Benedict's was a life in anthropology, and through that life we can understand with greater precision the life of anthropology itself as a living tradition, anthropology as a way of life. In *Patterns of Culture*, Ruth Benedict expressed her realization that the discipline of anthropology itself is a modern vision for a human way of being in the contemporary world.

Throughout her professional work one can see a creative tension, an impassioned tension, that centers on the evaluation of human experience, by examining her own experience in terms of common humanity. This same tension is to be found in her personal writings, her journals. Indeed, *Patterns of Culture* can only be understood fully if read as a personal statement. For, as a cultural relativist, Benedict had transcended the personal/professional distinction, and this transcendence was a major reason for the success of the book in introducing the thinking public to the significance of anthropology. To erase the personal/professional distinction in anthropology—whether in the classroom, library, or field, whether on the part of anthropologist or student—is not to replace objective fact with subjective fact, but to unify them in terms of a common humanity rooted in the discipline of empathy; it is to think, write, and act with fellow-feeling. A serious reading of *Patterns of Culture* begins with the realization that it is a modern, that is, natural, statement of self and social love in their unity. In the book Benedict expresses her love through affective description and a cultural discourse that exhibits not only thought but feeling. Such a humanistic anthropology is addressed to the willful creativity of humankind.

The first paragraph of the book invites the reader into the world of anthropology as into a world of appropriate description . . . history as human creativity. Human being is to be understood in terms of human behavior, and human behavior in terms of human creativity through time, culture as tradition rather than biology or race. "Anthropology is the study of human beings as creatures of *society*. It fastens its attention upon those physical characteristics and industrial techniques, those conventions and values, which *distinguish* one community from all others that belong to a different tradition" (1959:1, emphasis added). Benedict's discussions of human biology are limited to the contemplation of individual temperament conceived of as personal biological predispositions, and this only to stress the difficulties certain people may have in adjusting to certain ways of life into which they happen to be born. In *Patterns of Culture*, Benedict looks at what Edward Sapir, in his brilliant essay "Culture, Genuine and Spurious," called the "genuine culture" (1949:308–331), its apprehension as a creation of the moral imagination. But if culture so viewed is art, Benedict's goal is to cultivate not simply art appreciation but personal artistry as genuine human being and thus to bring the concept of culture to the level of individual — that is, personal — reality. To do so, she thinks of culture as human experience. Thus she introduces the consciousness of her readers to their cultural selves and thereby transforms human nature into cultural nature in all its varied forms, configurations, and patterns, each performed with exquisite idiosyncrasy by the human animals distinguished from all other animals by their intricate, subtle, and complex consciousnesses. By presenting anthropological knowledge as culture-consciousness and culture-consciousness as self-knowledge, she invites the reader simultaneously to look in and out, psychosocially, at human existence understood as the natural expression, the needful expression, of the human creative will, "values simply held" (Nadel 1953:272).

As this invitation is accepted, the doctrine of cultural relativism begins to make profound human sense. Benedict had always been concerned with what Philip Rieff (1979) has called the "parent question," To be or not to be?", but in its heroic or appropriately human phrasing: "How to be?" By understanding social life as the expression of human consciousness she came to understand moral being as a matter of human motivation and human motivation as a matter of values naturalistically understood. Benedict came to see anthropology as the teacher of values, for it had been her teacher. Her natural mind saw values as human creations. Values were apprehended as personal and social, psychosocial, in their derivation and sustenance — as creations of feeling. From her early childhood on, Ruth Benedict had been concerned with values and feelings in general as they manifest in social relationships, due in considerable part to her judgmental nature and her profound sense of being different from others. These concerns were intimately related as her need to judge deepened her sense of alienation. In cultural relativism she saw difference transformed into genius and genius into creativity, that is, into personal effort through time. She came to see human life as process and human selfhood — her own and that of her audience — as conscious moral being in the making, the process of making personal sense. She saw the unity of social development and self-development in cultural process, as a unity of human creativy. Her mature vision of anthropology thus became a vision of personal discipline or method, built on love, love being understood as the caring manifest in empathic understanding of self and other in the unity of common humanity. It is in this spirit that she invites us, in the final chapter of *Patterns of Culture,* to choose our "new normalities" (1959:271).

Ruth Benedict understood that, when we talk about morals specifically or values in general, we are talking about feelings. Such feelings, while they may be based on beliefs, are not themselves logico-empirically true or false, and in this sense are neither appropriate nor inappropriate. Rather they are empirically present or absent, in the sense of being personally and socially produced and experienced or not. She invites us to contemplate human life from this place of culture-consciousness as cultural animals, creative moral beings.

To study ethos is to study the emotional logic and human experience of a way of life through an interpretive description of that life in terms of values. Benedict realized that this was the proper way to present the doctrine of cultural relativism, for she realized that grappling with the problem of appropriate description was the primary task of culture theory. Only with affective understanding of the other, empathic understanding, could the self grow to modern human cultural maturity. Benedict saw modern maturity in terms of full culture-consciousness in the contemporary world. Only with affective understanding could naturalism turn to humanism and purely intellectual inquiry grow into a caring inquiry and description, into the art of anthropology as scientific humanism.

Patterns of Culture opens with a Digger Indian proverb: "In the beginning God gave to every people a cup of clay and from this cup they drank their life." Human life was not to be understood simply as molded existence, but rather, the very molds or cups were to be lovingly examined in terms of human consciousness so as to see the human lives they constituted. In this way Ruth Benedict hoped to bring about a new making, a new state of being, a culture-consciousness that would manifest itself in a changed way of life. It is for this reason that her book will always stand as a classic illustration of the teaching of anthropology as a human endeavor.

Benedict profoundly understood culture-consciousness and its vision of human realities as cultural realities—as stances toward life. As a humanist, she did not treat ways of life as answers to academic questions or as definitions of an external reality, as many scientistic culture theorists are prone to do. Rather she saw them as forming, as fashioning or creating, human experiential gestalts, ways of life. To look at human realities as cultural realities is to see them primarily as constitutive of human life worlds, not primarily as hypotheses regarding scientifically objective realities, as theorists such as Agassi and Jarvie (1967) would have it. She understood, as Roy Wagner does, the world of anthropology as itself a humanly created dimension of the human ecosystem. Thus her culture-talk in *Patterns of Culture* is a creative endeavor precisely in Wagner's sense of culture theory (Wagner 1975). She knew that to teach anthropology is to teach a type of thinking, a type of being, a method or discipline, in the process that is human life naturalistically understood. Benedict saw anthropology as empathy, as a method of comparative participant observation. Unlike many anthropologists, Ruth Benedict had a profound appreciation of the role of self-knowledge in comparative studies. She had a fundamental appreciation of the importance of participant observation in one's own life so as to enhance one's understanding and descriptions of the other. Benedict understood the personal or human dimension of the discipline, because it was the discipline through which she constituted her world. Thus she could write anthropology with feeling.

It is precisely this personal or human dimension that one must cultivate if one is to appreciate the doctrine of cultural relativism. It is this personal dimension that is needed for the profound cultivation of culture-consciousness. Culture-consciousness is the appreciation of common humanity—of basic human goodness—as a psychosocial making in all its creative dimensions, which we come to appreciate through the comparative method. This method, the road to self-knowledge through disciplined empathy, was Benedict's implicit understanding of the doctrine of cultural relativism. The concluding chapter of *Patterns of Culture* is called "The Individual and Culture." This title is significant because Benedict came to see this method as her working vision of the proper direction of human maturation. There is, in *Patterns of Culture*, a movement beyond the facts; a myth making, in terms of human feelings. This is precisely what distinguishes science from scientific humanism in anthropological culture theory. There is, in Benedict, an implicit conception of modern social maturation as a movement from empathic appreciation to mutual love, not inevitably but necessarily if human wellbeing is to be enhanced worldwide and personally. She understood love naturalistically, as a human making within a life seen as culture process.

To Ruth Benedict, anthropology was not only a way of understanding others, but simultaneously and necessarily, a way of reconstituting and/or cultivating self. This was to be accomplished by utilizing a new way of seeing other and self in the unity of empathy and self-knowledge, in common humanity.

Anthropology as the cultivation of common humanity is ruled by a first commandment that can be felt as a mirrored truth or emotional inverse: as we describe, so shall we be; and as we are, so shall we describe. To consciously seek to create human beauty within the dynamic tension of this circle of being is to practice anthropology as a personal moral discipline. The goal of the humanist is to move so deeply into the science that one recovers, acquires, and, most frequently, naturally cultivates one's common humanity—which, by the truth of our very social nature, must be shared. *Patterns of Culture* is such a sharing. It embodies Ruth Benedict's vision of anthropology as a human discipline, a social yet personal cultivation of common humanity through a primary identification as human being and a primary commitment to natural truth integrated in a natural moral discipline. Such a discipline, though of necessity personal, supports anthropology as human endeavor by substantially constituting its motivation.

In *Patterns of Culture*, Ruth Benedict displays the modern art of naturalistic moral description. She realized that value description is appropriate to self and other because it engages human beings in looking simultaneously inward and outward. It thereby naturally engages humanity in self-discovery through the quest for personal—that is, empathic—understanding of the other. In truth, as a humanist, Benedict was less concerned with the cup than with the affective and cognitive qualities of the drink of life it circumscribed. Thus she came to see moral issues as subject to naturalistic description in terms of human motivation and thus intuitively understood how to present the natural moral doctrine that is cultural relativism understood as scientific humanism. She understood from personal experience that the drink of life must be pleasurable, self-affirming. If not intoxicating, at least it must be worthwhile. She translated her alienation into value discourse. In the beginning of chapter 2 she relates the following interaction with an informant by the name of Ramon:

> One day, without transition, Ramon broke in upon his descriptions of grinding mesquite and preparing acorn soup. "In the beginning," he said, "God gave to every people a cup, a cup of clay, and from this cup they drank their life." I do not know whether the figure occurred in some traditional ritual of his people that I never found, or whether it was his own imagery. It is hard to imagine that he had heard it from the whites he had known at Banning; they were not given to discussing the ethos of different peoples. At any rate, in the mind of this humble Indian the figure of speech was clear and full of meaning. "They all dipped in the water," he continued, "but their cups were different. Our cup is broken now. It has passed away." (1959:21–22).

Benedict understood that Ramon was talking about the life of the human spirit, for she had searched personally for her cup in the modern world and had found it in the natural humanism of the doctrine of cultural relativism.

All of *Patterns of Culture* is a profound meditation on human motivation in relation to human ways of life. Benedict realized that cultural relativism was a natural moral doctrine that sought to study and cultivate the will to love, by appreciating others through natural human understanding and by cultivating self in the unity of human experience, through the comparative method. As Ruth Benedict came to see not only culture in general but love in particular as a human making rather than as a natural inclination or supernatural edit, she realized the importance of anthropology for the contemporary world. She saw serious engagement with the discipline as a self-development process at once personal and social, psychosocial. She saw it as an attempt lovingly to integrate affect and intellect by seeking the unity of self and other naturally but also lovingly—that is, appreciatively—in terms of common humanity. To see this is to understand more fully the significance of human dignity, respect, and tolerance in the world of anthropology constituted by the doctrine of cultural relativism. Thus Benedict sought to present cultural relativism as a synthesis of method and motivation, itself a fundamental aspect of a valued way of life.

Patterns of Culture is a human work of love. The doctrine of cultural relativism is a modern doctrine of emotional maturity. It views cultural absolutists as those who entertain feelings of certainty about issues that, when viewed from the crosscultural perspective, must be rendered tentative to the modern mind in the natural world. For example, what, if anything, happens to our spirit after death? Emotional certainty in such matters, when viewed from the perspective of culture-consciousness, indicates emotional immaturity in the modern world of cultural pluralism. If Ruth Benedict met Jerry Falwell, I'm sure she would treat him, at best, as an intellectual and emotional child who needs to grow up, for his own sake as well as for that of those around him.

It is love that renders Melville Herskovits' statements on the subject of cultural relativism philosophically confusing (Schmidt 1955). Herskovits talks about the doctrine as a method of human study, as a theory of knoweldge and a practical guide for moral being in the modern world, without adequately specifying the relationship between these various aspects of the doctrine. This gap arises because he is so anxious to arrive at tolerance in practice (Herskovits 1955). However, to say that cultural relativism is about human judgment is not to approach human judgment as a philosopher would.

The doctrine of cultural relativism begins by observing how human beings make judgments in cultural terms. It begins empirically at the level of "is", not the level of "ought." It accepts as natural the human tendency to judge negatively others who differ from oneself, just as it is natural to have an inflated self-image as a means of supporting positive self-judgment and affective being in general. Ethnocentrism flows from defensiveness, if not fear; but self-knowledge, if often not beautiful, allows one's respect for others to grow in the soil of one's own perceived inadequacies or affective deficiencies. It was Benedict's belief that the weaker the individual's immersion in a genuine or living cultural tradition, the greater the likelihood of a deeply-rooted negative sense of self. Often this type of emotional immaturity is morally if not psychologically appropriate, often it is not. In any case, it is likely to lead to fear that manifests itself in the extreme ethnocentrism of absolutists. In such persons ethnocentrism functions as the potent defensive mechanism of self-righteousness. Rather than appreciate the cultural or "value other," they focus on the other's differences with a highly negative attitude. In our immaturity, such focusing intensifies fear, which in turn heightens negative judgment.

From the perspective of culture-consciousness, we are far too judgmental because we are emotionally and cognitively immature. By seeing moral discourse as following scientific humanism, we can mature in our approach to contemporary issues of public concern which bear on tolerance and ethnocentrism. Such anthropological thought should be honored as a flowering of contemporary humanistic anthropology. Cultural relativism is a doctrine addressed to the customary mind in the contemporary world, and its message is that we are too judgmental in regard to the different and not judgmental enough in regard to the familiar and taken-for-granted.

It is precisely the caring manifest in the empathic understanding of self and other in the unity and equality of natural human being, cultural being, that provides the human logic, the affective and cognitive integration, that informs Benedict's presentation of the doctrine in *Patterns of Culture*. It is Ruth Benedict's empathy that makes of cultural relativism a modern doctrine of proper human love. She artfully employs an aesthetic naturalism that leads from the human science of anthropology to the scientific humanism, the naturalistic moral discourse, that is a uniquely modern possibility in humanistic anthropology. Ways of life are presented as paintings in a museum that come to life through the poetic sense of empathy. Absolutist judgments are transformed into preferences for certain styles or paintings in a museumlike atmosphere in which one cultivates personal appreciation for human creativity. Without realizing it, the reader comes to see ways of life as art, and cultural anthropology as the study of the art of living. Ranking one's favorite paintings at New York's Metropolitan Museum of Art in descending order of preference would be an absurd and misguided effort at self-cultivation. Ethnocentrism gradually is apprehended by the serious reader in a similar fashion. To destroy other ways of life is revealed as barbarism in the temple. Political and economic ideologies of one's own way of life are newly appreciated for their rationalizing rather than rational components.

Benedict's poetic being implicitly understood that to present the doctrine of cultural relativism properly, one must create a culture-talk of deep human feeling. *Pattern of Culture* is a presentation of anthropology as not only a scientific but also a spiritual discipline understood in its natural human unity. Benedict came to see anthropology as a unity of thought and feeling, as a cultural or creative endeavor that flows from natural human being in the contemporary world of anthropology constituted by those who practice the discipline. This is why cultural relativism makes good sense to many anthropologists.

Ruth Benedict had become a poet before she became an anthropologist, and her poetic being understood that self-reflexive naturalism, practiced with integrity in an atmosphere of freedom, nourishes the cultivation of humanism, naturally, of necessity. She understood this human truth to hold at both collective and individual levels of analysis. In this sense, the book can be read as a primer on the logic of cultural discourse as it applies to the individual and the group.

Fear and misunderstanding are truly the first enemies of self-knowledge; and self-forgiveness the first step in the journey of truthful understanding and loving of self and other in their unity. Mature, that is, self-informed, empathic understanding, as envisioned in the doctrine of cultural relativism, is not possible without the recognition that to understand all is to forgive all, not just in the world of scientific causation but in the world of naturalistic moral discourse as well. Benedict came to understand the relationship between forgiving other and forgiving self in a unified and dignified way, through the disciplined cultivation of common humanity in anthropology. It is not simply that we must understand before we can judge but rather that the very human process of understanding changes our judgments, just as self-knowledge changes our concerns. Indeed, naturalistic moral discourse in anthropology can be said to commence when we seek the moral limits of empathy. But to seek its limits we must first understand its vast domain in the world of human understanding.

Like Socrates, Benedict realized the relationship between self-knowledge and social ethics, between thought and behavior. But whereas Socrates thought he was talking to the gods, Benedict realized she was talking to and about herself, psychosocially interpreted through her artful description of the cultural other. She understood the doctrine of cultural relativism not only as a social ethic but also as a teaching about how to look at yourself, cultivate yourself, and live from your feelings as integrated with your modern mind in a life discipline that is a modern moral being in the world. To Benedict, cultural relativism was a psychosocial ideal, a sense of direction in the contemporary world of humanity. Thus she found in the doctrine a way of making personal sense that was available to the disaffected modern mind.

Melville Herskovits stated the principal of cultural relativism as follows: "Judgments are based on experience and experience is *interpreted* by each individual in terms of his own enculturation" (1955:351, emphasis added). He hoped that a cognitive appeal to human reason would further naturalistic moral discourse. Benedict, however, realized that all too often cognitive interpretations ultimately serve affective needs. She realized, as only one involved in lifelong self-study could, that an appeal to intellect must fight off natural emotional tendencies to rationalize rather than to reason.

In *Patterns of Culture* Ruth Benedict sought to minimize such ethnocentrism by artfully constituting empathic understanding through empathic description. An example is her citation of Nietzsche in her characterization of the Pueblos:

> The basic contrast between the Pueblos and the other cultures of North America is the contrast that is named and described by Nietzsche in his studies of Greek tragedy. He discusses two diametrically opposed ways of arriving at the values of existence. The Dionysian pursues them through "the annihilation of the ordinary bounds and limits of existence"; he seeks to attain in his most valued moments escape from the boundaries imposed upon him by his five senses, to break through into another order of experience. The desire of the Dionysian, in personal experience or in ritual, is to press through it toward a certain psychological state, to achieve excess. The closest analogy to the emotions he seeks is drunkenness, and he values the illuminations of frenzy. With Blake, he believes "the path of excess leads to the palace of wisdom." The Apollonian distrusts all this, and has often little idea of the nature of such experiences. He finds means to outlaw them from his conscious life. He "knows but one law, measure in the Hellenic sense." He keeps the middle of the road, stays within the psychological states. In Nietzsche's fine phrase, even in the exaltation of the dance he "remains what he is, and retains his civic name."
>
> The Southwest Pueblos are Appollonian. Not all of Nietzsche's discussion of the contrast between Appollonian and Dionysian applies to the contrast between the Pueblos and the surrounding peoples. The fragments I have quoted are faithful descriptions, but there were refinements of the types in Greece that do not occur among the Indians of the Southwest, and among these latter, again, there are refinements that did not occur in Greece. It is with no thought of equating the civilization of Greece with that of aboriginal America that I use, in describing the cultural configurations of the latter, terms borrowed from the culture of Greece. I use them because they are categories that bring clearly to the fore the major qualities that differentiate Pueblo culture from those of other American Indians, not because all the attitudes that are found in Greece are found also in aboriginal America. (1959:78–79)

Only after the human experience of empathic understanding of the cultural other, only after naturalism grows into an embracing humanism, love in its anthropological phrasings, could interpretation based on common humanity—human nature in its natural moral forms understood psychosocially—be plausible to the customary mind. It is ironic how difficult the customary mind finds it to understand conformity to different cultural traditions, but this irony is at the heart of a human understanding of ethnocentrism. Benedict understood that love of human being, while not necessary for anthropology as science, *was* necessary for an understanding of the human significance of the doctrine of cultural relativism as a natural psychosocial moral doctrine.

To appreciate the poetry of *Patterns of Culture*, one must see it as flowing from this creative realization of human being as affective being. Its principal of cultural relativism may be stated as follows: "Judgments of cultural difference should flow from feelings of human sameness." Differences in human ways of life are intimately related to socially created feelings, and how you feel about others is in profound ways an outward manifestation of how you feel about yourself. While it is true that to understand all is to forgive all, the more axiomatic psychosocial truth is that pragmatically nonessential empathic understanding — that which is not necessary for your own adaptation and survival — is a matter of choice. As such, it is the expression of love in its deepest anthropological sense: social love as a willingness to suffer for others. To identify with others involves a sharing of their joys as well as their sufferings. But a deepened sensitivity to human sociality itself, leads to a deepened sense of human sensitivity and vulnerability and thus of human suffering in general. Benedict understood the great — indeed, heroic — creative achievement that is human normality in any of its various cultural configurations. She was acutely aware of the human creation of human suffering. Thus she appreciated that the unconditional recognition that the other exists in equal moral value to the self, and the acceptance and cultivation of "human being" as one's primary natural identity, are the first steps towards thinking, feeling, and acting from culture-consciousness — a natural understanding of human ways of life in their creative equality. As a culture-conscious being she could appreciate how our naturally essential sociality, heightened and focused as it is through enculturation, could, particularly in cases of absolutist enculturation, lead to virulent forms of ethnocentrism generative of substantial and unnecessary human suffering. Through her aesthetic naturalism, her search for human beauty in the synthesis of the pleasurable and morally correct, she sought to vivify cultural relativism by practicing the high art of naturally truthful but compassionate description. She wished to cultivate the natural love of common humanity by identifying human creativity with the moral imagination empathetically understood through value description. This is the root—or, as we say in the Bronx, the bottom line—of her concept of culture-consciousness (see Geertz 1983).

To enter the world of cultural relativism, to cross the threshold from partial empathic understanding to total or self-identificatory understanding, is a matter of lifelong choice, a conscious cultivation of a modern character understood in terms of spirit, of motivation. Humanistic anthropology begins with the study of other as self-in-another-form. Ruth Benedict chose to place her faith in the modern world of anthropology, the world of common humanity understood as Konrad Lorenz understood it:

> Always and everywhere it is the unreasoning, emotional appreciation of values that adds a plus or a minus sign to the answer of Kant's categorical self-questioning and makes it an imperative or a veto. By itself, reason can only devise means to achieve otherwise determined ends; it cannot set up goals or give us orders. Left to itself, reason is like a computer into which no relevant information conducive to an important answer has been fed; logically valid though all its operations may be, it is a wonderful system of wheels within wheels, without a motor to make them go round (Lorenz 1967:240).

Ruth Benedict understood that the study of human being as social being through a psychosocial, identificatory, empathic understanding itself was a social act with psychosocial consequences for self and other in their mutuality. This comprehension is exhibited from the first paragraph of her book to the last. It is exhibited from her revealing reference to "the scale of human values" (1959:247), to her discussions of homosexuals and American family life. Throughout these discussions the unvoiced question that serves as methodological guide in her value inquiries is always the same: "How would *you* feel if . . . ?" In this way *Patterns of Culture* naturally moves from a discussion of human nature to a discussion of common humanity, moral being in the crosscultural or modern world.

As a young girl and indeed into early adolescence, Ruth Benedict was given to fits of anger and violence. Sociality never came easily to her. But, like the primitive shaman before her, she turned personal suffering into personal growth through serving others. As late as 1926, at the age of thirty-nine, she wrote in her journal:

> This mood that haunts me with such persistency has nothing to do with any nihilism. It passes for such, but it's really a refuge from it. I know to the bottom of my subconsciousness that no combination of circumstances, no love, no well-being, will ever give me what I want. But death will. Passion is a turn-coat, but death will endure always; life is a bundle of fetters or it isn't worth living, and for all our dreaming of freedom, only death can give it to us. Life must be always demeaning itself, but death comes with dignity we don't have even to deserve. We all know these things but in me it's bred a passionate conviction that death is better than life. Why do people fear and resent it? Shouldn't they hanker for it? Isn't it good to know that we'll be the plowed earth of this planet through hot generations that will disport themselves as we did, millions of ants upon their ant hill?
>
> And my mood has nothing to do with suicide. It's a cheap way of attaining death, and death at least need not come cheap. I shall come by it honestly, and I wish I could think that people would feel that same honor for me that I feel first at any news of death — the honor for anyone who has held out to the end. (Mead 1959a:154–55)

The extent of her emotional maturation can be gauged by comparing this self-relevation with what she *chose* to write as the concluding paragraph of *Patterns of Culture* and realizing that the latter statement does not imply the personal negation of the former:

> Social thinking at the present time has no more important task before it than that of taking adequate account of cultural relativity. In the fields of both sociology and psychology the implications are fundamental, and modern thought about contacts of peoples and about our changing standards is greatly in need of sane and scientific direction. The sophisticated modern temper has made of social relativity, even in the small area which it has recognized, a doctrine of despair. It has pointed out its incongruity with the orthodox dreams of permanence and ideality and with the individual's illusions of autonomy. It has argued that if human experience must give up these, the nutshell of existence is empty. But to interpret our dilemma in these terms is to be guilty of an anachronism. It is only the inevitable cultural lag that makes us insist that the old must be discovered again in the new, that there is no solution but to find the old certainty and stability in the new plasticity. The recognition of cultural relativity carries with it its own values, which need not be those of the

absolutist philosophies. It challenges customary opinions and causes those who have been bred to them acute discomfort. It rouses pessimism because it throws old formulas into confusion, not because it contains anything intrinsically difficult. As soon as the new opinion is embraced as customary belief, it will be another trusted bulwark of the good life. We shall arrive then at a more realistic social faith, accepting as grounds of hope and as new bases for tolerance the coexisting and equally valid patterns of life which mankind has created for itself from the raw materials of experience. (1959:278)

As William Wordsworth wrote: "In spite of differences of soil and climate, of language and manners, of laws and customs—in spite of things silently gone out of mind, and things violently destroyed, the Poet binds together by passion and knowledge the vast empire of human society as it is spread over the whole earth, and over all time" (*Poetical Works*, ed. Selincourt, 1940). Such a binding is the doctrine of cultural relativism as presented in the book *Patterns of Culture*. This book exhibits the spirit of anthropology, humanistically understood as the social yet personal study of the cultural other and the cultural self in their mutualities as biographies in history. This interpretive anthropology is the human act of personal sensemaking.

I have faith that, consciously and well, we can study and teach scientific humanism in anthropology. I have faith that many of our students will understand. For I have an abiding personal faith in common humanity as our most precious primitive—that is, minimally human (see Diamond 1974)—key to survival.

3 Biography and Natural Moral Being: The Teaching of Anthropology

In his wonderful book, *A Little Boy in Search of God: Mysticism in a Personal Light*, Issac Bashevis Singer writes of his personal attempt to make sense of human experience. He was attempting to reconcile his growing knowledge of the Jewish mysticism of the Cabala with his dawning awareness of scientific knowledge:

> My moods varied swiftly. Now I was in ecstasy and soon deep in despair. The cause of my gloom was often the same — unbearable pity for those who were suffering and who had suffered in all the generations. I had heard about the cruelties perpetrated by Chmielnicki's Cossacks. I had read about the Inquisition. I knew about the pogroms on Jews in Russia and Spain. I lived in a world of cruelty. I was tormented not only by the sufferings of men but by the sufferings of beasts, birds, and insects as well. Hungry wolves attacked lambs. Lions, tigers, and leopards had to devour other creatures or die from hunger. The squires wandered through forests and shot deer, hares, and pheasants for pleasure. I bore resentment not only against man but against God, too. It was He who had provided the savage beasts with claws and fangs. It was He who had made man a bloodthirsty creature ready to do violence at every step. I was a child, but I had the same view of the world that I have today — one hugh slaughterhouse, one enormous hell. (1976:49)

As I reread these words, written by the great writer at the age of seventy-one years, I realized that I too formed my sense of the world at an early age.

I was born in 1943 to second generation Jewish-American parents in New York City. I was raised in a moral tradition so deep that it was taken for granted, as is the case in many primitive societies. When I was a small child, Adolf Hitler was, in my mind, the devil incarnate, the very personification of evil. Every night I would say my "Now I lay me down to sleep." I would say goodnight to all the good people in the world and pray that God would preserve their lives through the night and make the bad people good so that I could say goodnight to everyone in the world.

I distinctly remember, at the age of seven or eight, leaving my family's apartment on the second floor of a six-story building in the East Bronx and heading excitedly for the street to play with my buddies. As fate would have it, my apartment was right at the head of the stairs. As I turned to descend, in anxious anticipation of "hitting the street," I missed the top step and fell head-over-heels down the long flight of marble and iron stairs in my once-elegant apartment building. When I hit the bottom, I railed at God for treating a nice little boy so shabbily. As I reread Singer's line, "I was a child, but I had the same view of the world that I have today—one huge slaughterhouse, one enormous hell," I realized for the first time that when I hit the bottom of the stairs, I became an anthropologist, though I would not know it or be able to name it for another decade.

I remember that, as I was rolling down the staircase, I was saying to myself that I hoped I wouldn't get badly hurt—break my head, as it were. When I hit the bottom, more or less in one piece, I praised my good fortune, vented my anger, and set out to have a good time in the bright sunlight of that New York City morning. Reading Singer reminded me that my trip down the stairs was a rather clumsy "rite of passage." Philip Rieff was fond of observing, in his National Endowment for the Humanities seminar on "Art and Society," Plato's sense of wisdom was the experience of being reminded. By the time I had hit the bottom of those stairs, Adolf Hitler had become not the devil, but just a human being, in a human history capable of producing Christs and Hitlers, tyrants and sufferers. At that point, unbeknownst to me, I had become a pilgrim in search of a new moral tradition, a moral tradition that I found in anthropology and have come to call scientific humanism.

After many years of teaching, I have realized that anthropology as science is only part of a larger anthropological tradition, anthropology as humanism. I have come to know humanism by seeing anthropology as a moral tradition rooted in natural truth and the natural human abilities to creatively express love. It is the moral ethos of anthropology that renders the discipline meaningful to many students and compelling to many professional anthropologists.

To mask this moral discipline in a Weberian distinction between the scientist and the politician, or in a distinction between two cultures, the sciences and the humanities, in the fashion of C.P. Snow, is to render the teaching of anthropology trivial in a profound sense, the sense in which knowing anthropology or not makes a significant human difference.

F.R. Leavis, in his wonderful essay, "Two Cultures? The Significance of C.P. Snow," notes, "In coming to terms with great literature, we discover what at bottom we really believe. What for—what ultimately for? What do men live by—the questions work and tell at what I can only call a religious depth of thought and feeling" (1963:43). Surely the same is potentially true of learning anthropology. This shared truth has implications for how to think about doing and reporting anthropological research and, at least of equal importance, for teaching anthropology. Leavis is speaking of a moral depth that is not coterminous with religion. Intellectually speaking, this is why the Religious Right sees "secular humanism" as its enemy. But "secular humanism," if it has any validity as a category, is synonymous with the life of, and faith in, the human mind and its creative capacities to adapt and adjust to human truth—that is, natural truth.

To teach anthropology humanistically is to teach with feeling, to teach with the integrity of personal example. To teach humanistically is to teach with the realization that what one teaches is important precisely because it is important to oneself, not as answer but as opportunity. As naturalistic understanding precedes action for the contemporary mind, so empathy must precede but not exclude moral judgment in anthropology.

A number of years ago, when the American Anthropological Association passed a motion against "creation science," the motion talked about the inappropriateness of this approach in a science class. But the action specifically limited the group's condemnation, failing to censure the doctrine as inappropriate for teaching in any institution of higher learning. In stopping short, the AAA echoed the compromise that science historically has made with religion, a compromise that can be understood in terms of pragmatics rather than in terms of integrity. As Jacob Bronowski noted in regard to the trial of Galileo:

Galileo seems to me to have been strangely innocent about the world of politics, and most innocent in thinking that he could outwit it because he was clever. For twenty years and more he moved along a path that led inevitably to his condemnation. It took a long time to undermine him; but there was never any doubt that Galileo would be silenced, because the division between him and those in authority was absolute. They believed that faith should dominate; and Galileo believed that truth should persuade" (1973:205).

From this observation we can pass with greater appreciation to Ruth Benedict's declaration on the final page of *Patterns of Culture*, "The recognition of cultural relativity carries with it its own values, which need not be those of the absolutist philosophies" (1959:278). Those values are the values of science itself which potentially can be appreciated in anthropology, a science *of* self, as in no other scientific discipline. To teach anthropology humanistically is fully to confront the human significance of contemporary, naturalistic, or scientific truth with an integrity that approaches Galileo's innocence. To avoid such confrontation is to trivialize the discipline into the subjective appreciation of exotica or to rationalize it upon the basis of a quest for a scientific technology of the psychosocial that will never, and indeed should never, be realized.

To teach anthropology humanistically is to practice scientific humanism in the classroom in a manner demanded of no other science educator. For in anthropology, science's self-reflective nature is heightened so as to bring not only the observed, but the observer under self-scrutiny.

Teaching anthropology humanistically must involve a sharing of one's own efforts at making personal sense so as to communicate the human significance of the discipline. Teaching anthropology involves the professor in the personal development of a philosophical anthropology that we would do well to recognize in each of our courses. To do this, we must explore the humanistic and naturalistic roots of science itself as a human endeavor, in all complex unities. Unities that are themselves constitutive of a moral vision of human being, reflective of a world view. Ruth Benedict wrote that "culture provides the raw material of which the individual makes his life" (1959:251–52). Does not anthropology stand in the same relationship to its students, seen as personal sensemakers? To realize that absolutists are the enemy requires a moral vision—the moral vision of scientific humanism, of naturalistic moral discourse—that is uniquely contemporary in its rejection of doctrinnaire preaching and power.

To teach and study humanistic anthropology is not to abandon faith, or artificially to separate it from intellectual inquiry, but to rethink it and replace it in one's hierarchy of values, below truth. Scientific humanism is committed to exploring the relationship between "is" and "ought."

Jerry Falwell and the so-called Religious Right display more integrity in their attacks on "secular humanism" than did the American Anthropological Association in its condemnation of the teaching of "creation science" in the science classroom. For Falwell realizes, as do many religious reactionaries, that scientific humanism, this reshaping of the human spirit and perspective, is a hermeneutic equivalent of his supernatural belief. Nowhere is this more true than in the science of anthropology. As Isaac Bashevis Singer intuitively realized as a young boy, science and religion must be in dialogue if either is to remain vital in the contemporary life of the free mind, the self-creative or contemporary mind, the liberal imagination. The place for such dialogue is the domain of scientific humanism; a domain in which "is" and "ought" are not viewed as mutually exclusive isolates but rather as stages in a unified process of natural moral discourse that seeks to cultivate the personal discovery of common humanity as a road to personal wellbeing. In the final analysis, this is the heart of anthropology's rightful place in the teachings that constitute the contemporary liberal arts tradition. It is the science in which one can discover one's humanity.

To teach culture humanistically is to teach the integrity of the contemporary life of the mind as an invitation to self-exploration. To teach in this way is to present the science of anthropology as a prelude to a mature making of personal sense. It is to teach anthropology as scientific humanism, a world view that is a method of seeing and being in their unity, as a vehicle for human maturation—a sense of direction rather than a set of directions.

When we see the intersections of humanism and naturalism in the science of the human, we will appreciate anthropology as scientific humanism, itself a world view and a way of life. This metacultural system Ruth Benedict tried existentially to capture in the term culture-consciousness. It is only from the realization of culture-consciousness that the theories and human strivings of anthropologists and anthropology can be appreciated by students as personal endeavor. Anthropology is itself a particular cultural reality, and, as cultural relativists have realized, it, like any constitution of the beautiful, must simultaneously constitute its ugly, the absolutists.

The faith of anthropology, like all faiths, has its degree of affect as well as intellect, and it is for this reason that it must be placed beneath truth. The critic of the Third Reich and of Adolf Hitler's vision must begin with their falseness, not their evilness. Evil is a moral category, and in the modern world of dawning natural moral discourse, in which humanistic anthropology is to play a vital part, truth must supercede goodness if intellect rather than affect, and adaptation that is not illusory, are to guide the inevitable expressions of the human spirit. It is this stance which distinguishes us from Dostoevsky's Grand Inquisitor and unites us with his Christ. Contemporary anthropology is based on a world view that allows multiple theories and practices, for it is nourished by the value of tolerance that grows through reflexive and self-reflective understanding.

I shall conclude by describing how I begin my introductory courses in cultural anthropology. I quote a statement by Robert Redfield from "Changing Ethical Judgment," the concluding chapter of his book *The Primitive World and Its Transformations*: "I cannot prove to you that man should act more decently and more humanely" (1953:164). I then invite my students to prove it to themselves by studying the science of anthropology so as to cultivate their own humanity. I invite them to become participant observers in their own lives, so as to realize the meaning of culture-consciousness.

SECTION II

4   Magic, Science, and Religion

This essay is an examination of a conceptual tradition in the anthropology of religion. I shall be discussing the ideas of three leading figures in anthropology: Edward Burnett Tylor, who many identify as the founder of modern anthropology; Sir James George Frazer, who may well have been the most famous British anthropologist; and Bronislaw Malinowski, who is among the first ranks of twentieth-century anthropologists and, along with his archrival Radcliffe-Brown, cofounder of the functionalist school of anthropology. I have chosen to consider the ideas of these three anthropologists not because of their lasting merit, though students of anthropology can still learn humility by familiarizing themselves with the life work of these great scholars. Rather, it is my assertion that their endeavors have implications for the continued development of cultural anthropology and possibly, as I will indicate at the end of this discussion, for understanding contemporary society. There have been many helpful ideas regarding magic and religion since Malinowski's time. Nevertheless, the tradition, initiated at the beginning of modern anthropology, that viewed these two categories of cultural existence in relation to science, continues to provides a clear indication of anthropology's treatment of the nonrational in human life.

Eric Wolf, an eminent American anthropologist, has stated that "for the first time in human history, we have transcended the inherited divisions of the human phenomenon into segments of time and segments of space" (1964:95). He was reflecting on the wealth of anthropological materials related to prehistoric peoples, to nonliterate hunting and gathering peoples living in small societies with simple material artifacts, to Neolithic tribal populations, and to archaic and contemporary peasant and urban peoples. Anthropology has been, and continues to be, a discipline devoted to relating to other ways of life. It is in the context of this central concern of anthropology that I am writing.

Marvin Harris, in his masterly work *The Rise of Anthropological Theory*, makes clear that the earliest anthropological strategy for relating to other ways of life was to propound a theory of racial determinism under the guise of science. "According to the doctrine of scientific racism, the significant socio-cultural differences and similarities among human populations are the dependent variables of group-restricted hereditary drives and attitudes" (1968:81). Supposed hereditary components were freely attributed and shaped into whatever quantity or quality of influence was necessary to account for the "peculiarities" under consideration. Even Lewis Henry Morgan, considered by many the founder of modern American anthropology and its leading figure in the nineteenth century, was capable of the following statement:

> There are some customs of such a strikingly personal character that they may in a preeminent degree, be regarded as customs of the blood. When prevalent over wide areas and persistently maintained from generation to generation, they seem to possess some significance upon the question of the probable genetic connection of the peoples by whom they are practiced. There are three distinct customs or usages of this character, apparently transmitted with the blood, which I have taken some pains to trace, and have found them to be substantially universal in the Ganowanian family. They may posses some value as corroborative evidence of the unity of origin of these nations. These are, first, the custom of saluting by kin; second, the usage of wearing the breech-cloth; and third, the usage of sleeping at night in a state of nudity, each person being wrapped in separate covering. (Harris 1968:138)

Similar statements by such eminent nineteenth-century students of humanity as Herbert Spencer and Edward Burnett Tylor could be cited (see Harris 1968:130, 140). Nevertheless, the work of such scholars as these gradually led to the predominance of a different anthropological manner of relating to other ways of life.

Spencer's concept of the superorganic, Durkheim's concepts of the social fact and collective representations, and, most importantly for American anthropology, Tylor's concept of culture, helped bring about the predominance of this alternate conceptual framework. Tylor's concept of culture, freed of its racial associations largely through the efforts of the great American anthropologist Franz Boas and his students, including Ruth Benedict, Margaret Mead, and Ashley

Montague, has served as a foundation for modern cultural anthropology. This conceptual framework views man as possessing, on the one hand, quite generalized and inadequate innate behavioral capacities and, on the other, astonishing intellectual and creative capabilities. It has focused on the development, manifestation, alteration, and transmission of learned traditions. To quote Tylor's classic definition, "culture . . . is that complex whole which includes knowledge, belief, art, law, morals, custom and any other capabilities and habits acquired by man as a member of society" (1871:1). As Alfred Kroeber and Clyde Kluckhohn point out, "The specifically anthropological concept [of culture] crystallized first around the idea of 'custom.' Then . . . custom was given a time backbone in the form of 'tradition' or social heritage" (1952:67). These two eminent anthropologists, as part of a study critically reviewing literally hundreds of anthropological definitions of the term *culture*, offer the following as an attempted consensus definition: "Culture consists of patterns of and for behavior acquired and transmitted by symbols, constituting the distinctive achievements of human groups, including their embodiments in artifacts; the essential core of culture consists of traditional (historically derived and selected) ideas and especially their attached values" (1952:66). This definition reflects the fact that, in American anthropology, the conceptualization of culture emphasizes the notion of "collective mental life," an aspect of what disparagingly has been labeled "cultural idealism" (Harris 1968).

Other ways of life now could be considered as specimens of culture, subtype Trobriand Islands or Cheyenne Indians or Iglulik Eskimos. Obviously this definition did not eliminate the problem of relating to the significantly different ways of life; it simply changed the terminology and indicated a new explanatory strategy. The cultures of many of the nonliterate, small-scale societies with simple material artifacts (by our current cultural standards) appeared to be quite different from the cultures of American and British anthropologists. Western anthropologists were steeped in the dogmas of intellectualism, evolutionism, utilitarianism, and scientism. They were committed to a faith in the inevitability of continual progress. They were convinced that this progress would take the form of materially-induced improvement in the human condition. Such factors, along with a troubling incapacity to resist scaling difference along some continuum of better to worse, led many to view nonliterate peoples as ignorant and superstitious. The provincialism of the natives, along with their lack of appreciation of Western culture, probably contributed to this tendency. The problem of coming to terms with other ways of life thus in large measure was transformed into the problem of coming to terms with ignorance and superstition. It should be noted that another highly successful technique for coming to terms with the different was being applied simultaneously by those with less than academic interest—namely, destroying it. I shall return to this point.

In attempting to understand the supposed ignorance and superstition embodied in other peoples' ways of life, Western anthropologists made a significant and, in my opinion, unfortunate association; they decided that these peoples all had "religions." For the vast majority of late-nineteenth-century and twentieth-century anthropologists, the most significant domain of ignorance and superstition in their own societies' ways of life was a group of beliefs, attitudes, behaviors, and institutions named by the natives—in this case participants in Western culture—"religion." Thus, relating to the ways of life of many nonliterate cultures became in part the province of the anthropology of "primitive religion." E.E. Evans-Pritchard, the great British social anthropologist, speaking of the eminent theorists of "primitive religion" in his book *The Theories of Primitive Religion*, states:

> If one is to understand the interpretations of primitive mentality they put forward, one has to know their own mentality, broadly where they stood; to enter into their way of looking at things, a way of their class, sex, and period. As far as religion goes, they all had, as far as I know, a religious background in one form or another. To mention some names which are most likely to be familiar to you: Tylor had been brought up a Quaker, Frazer a Presbyterian, Marett in the Church of England, Malinowski a Catholic, while Durkheim, Levy-Bruhl, and Freud had a Jewish background; but with one or two exceptions, whatever the background may have been, the persons whose writings have been most influential have been at the time they wrote agnostics or atheists. Primitive religion was with regard to its validity no different from any other religious faith, an illusion. It was not just that they asked, as Bergson put it, how it is that "beliefs and practices which are anything but reasonable could have been and still are, accepted by reasonable beings." It was rather that implicit in their thinking were the optimistic convictions of the eighteenth-century

rationalist philosophers that people are stupid and bad only because they had bad institutions, and they have bad institutions only because they are ignorant and superstitious, and they are ignorant and superstitious because they have been exploited in the name of religion by cunning and avaricious priests and the unscrupulous classes which have supported them. (1965:14, 15)

Previously, in his *Aquinas Lecture of 1959,*" Evans-Pritchard had observed:

> Among the last generation of distinguished American anthropologists there was not one, as far as I know, who gave assent to any creed, unless agnosticism be accounted one, or who regard all religious belief as other than illusion, and I do not know of a single person among the prominent sociologists and anthropologists of America at the present time who adheres to any faith. Religion is superstition to be explained by anthropologists, not something an anthropologist, or indeed any rational person, could himself believe in. (1952:162)

Curiously if not unexpectedly, rather than studying the beliefs, attitudes, and practices of the members of small-scale societies as social facts and focusing on their relationship to other social facts, with few exceptions the classic theorists deemed it necessary to investigate so-called primitive religion by devising explanations of its origin. These origin theories they believed would account for the essential features of all so-called religions. Many students of humankind were motivated by the desire to discredit religion in their own society. It is from this insight that we can understand why many of the classic anthropological perspectives on primitive man seem to many contemporary theorists to be inadequate, ludicrous, and downright unscientific.

Let us now turn to the specific formulations of Tylor, Frazer, and Malinowski. The theories of Tylor and Frazer have been categorized by Evans-Pritchard, following Wilhelm Schmidt, as "psychological—subcategory intellectualist" (1965:4) and by Annemarie de Waal Malefijt as "rationalistic." As Malefijt observed, "Rationalism is the acceptance of human reason as the ultimate source of knowledge. Applied to the nineteenth-century study of religion, it meant the conviction that prehistoric humankind reasoned out his beliefs in an almost scientific manner, but arrived at the wrong conclusions because he lacked knowledge and experience and the opportunity for scientific observation" (1968:48).

Edward Tylor (1832–1917) was described as "tall, handsome as a Greek god, gentle at heart, and at the same time possessing the hard, keen, penetrating intelligence of the naturalist of genius" (Hays 1964: 63). His father was a wealthy, liberal Quaker who owned a brass foundry. After completing grammar school, he entered the family business, but, threatened with tuberculosis, he came to the United States for a beneficial change in climate. Eventually he visited Cuba and from there went on to Mexico, where his devotion to what he termed the "science of ethnology" developed. His major works include *Researches into the Early History of Mankind and the Development of Civilization* (1865), *Primitive Culture* (1871), and *Anthropology: An Introduction to the Study of Man and Civilization* (1881), the first textbook in anthropology.

In trying to analyze nonliterate cultures, Tylor made use of the concepts "magic," "science," and "religion." He reasoned that early humankind, reflecting on such experiences as death, disease, trance, visions, and, most importantly, dreams, had come to the conclusion that such phenomena were to be accounted for by the presence or absence of an immaterial entity, the soul. As Tylor stated:

> It seems as though thinking men, as yet at a low level of culture, were deeply impressed by two groups of biological problems. In the first place, what is it that makes the difference between a living body and a dead one; what causes waking, sleep, trance, disease, death? In the second place, what are those human shapes which appear in dreams and visions? Looking at these two groups of phenomena, the ancient savage philosophers probably made their first step by the obvious inference that every man has two things belonging to him, namely, a life and a phantom. These two are evidently in close connection with the body, the life as enabling it to feel and think and act, the phantom as being its image or second self . . . They are doctrines answering in the most forcible way to the plain evidence of men's senses, as interpreted by a fairly consistent and rational primitive philosophy. (Lessa and Vogt 1965:13)

Souls being detachable from whatever they were inhabiting were thus thought of as independent of their material homes, leading, according to Tylor, to the idea of spiritual beings. Tylor's minimum definition of religion was "the belief in Spiritual Beings," a level he called *animism.* Analogous beliefs and practices in literate cultures he considered to be "survivals" retained by force of habit.

Starting with animism, Tylor proceeded to trace what he considered to be an evolutionary development. First, the belief in souls was extended to include animals, plants, and inanimate objects, since they too appeared in dreams. The development of communal ritual came about, according to Tylor, with the appearance of ancestor-worship. He reasoned that early man believed the soul to be superior to the body, since it survived the body, had physical power, and could move quickly. After death the souls became what he termed "manes," whose powers were first admired and then worshipped: "The dead ancestor, now passed into a deity, simply goes on protecting his own family and receiving suit and service from them as of old; the dead chief still watches over his own tribe, still holds the authority by helping friends and harming enemies, still rewards the right and sharply punishes the wrong" (Malefijt 1968:50). From there Tylor went on to account for the development of what he considered to be the various other religious phenomena, by continually attributing to early humankind the development of a number of theories, which he termed *doctrines*. Eventually he accounted for such supposed categories of religious phenomena as fetishism, polytheism, and monotheism in an evolutionary sequence.

Tylor treated what he termed "magic" separately from religion, describing the latter as "this farrago of nonsense."* Nevertheless, his approach emphasized the element of reason. To Tylor, "magic" was based on observation and classification of similarities, the first essential process in human knowledge: "As yet in a low intellectual condition [man] having come to associate in thought those things which he found by experience to be connected in fact, proceeded erroneously to invert this action, and to conclude that association in thought must involve connection in reality" (Wax and Wax 1963:495). Tylor went on to give a number of reasons why the futility of magic would not be discovered by the people who believed in it:

1) Nature or the magician's trickery often brought about the desired results;

---

*According to Evans-Pritchard, Tylor distinguished magic "from religion rather for convenience of exposition than on grounds of aetiology or validity" (1965:26)

2) Failure to carry out some procedure correctly or to observe some proscription could be blamed:
3) Countermagic could be blamed;
4) Success or failure is not always clear;
5) People are prone to be more aware of positive evidence supported by authority than of negative contradictory evidence (Evans-Pritchard 1965:27).

Sir James G. Frazer (1854–1941), the next major figure in this tradition, came from a family of prosperous Glasgow merchants and was educated at Trinity College, Cambridge University. Originally interested in classical Greece, his career took a significant turn when a friend gave him a copy of Tylor's book, *Primitive Culture*. Frazer later stated publicly that he owed his interest in anthropology to Tylor and had been greatly influenced by Tylor's ideas. His most famous work, *The Golden Bough*, published between 1890 and 1915 in thirteen volumes, reflected scholarship, great industry, and, I suspect, a dearth of outside diversions. His other works include *Totemism and Exogamy* (1910), *Folklore in the Old Testament* (1918), and *The Fear of the Dead in Primitive Religion* (1935).

Frazer added only one completely new element to Tylor's formulations, that of stages of human intellectual development. According to Frazer, mankind everywhere sooner or later must pass through three stages of intellectual development: from magic, in which man is superstitious instead of rational, to religion; and from religion to science. In contrast to Tylor, but along with many other scholars of his time, Frazer believed that so-called magic preceded so-called religion. Frazer reasoned that, at some stage in the human career, some shrewd fellows must have discovered that magic didn't work, but being unable to overcome their impotence by empirical means nor live philosophically with their limitations, they fell into the second grand illusion, i.e., that there were spiritual beings who could aid them. These higher powers were appealed to with offerings, sacrifices, verbal flattery, and appeals. Finally, the bogus nature of spirits was seen, and experimental science was born.

The other elaboration by Frazer on Tylor's formulation concerns the former's treatment of the supposed similarity of science and magic. Tylor had termed magic "an elaborate and systematic pseudo-science" but had failed to go into any systematic analysis of this formulation (Wax and Wax 1963:495). Frazer did just that, stating that magic was a phenomenon whose "fundamental conception is identical with that of modern science: underlying the whole system is a faith, implicit but real and firm, in the order and uniformity of nature. . . . One event follows another necessarily and inevitably, without the intervention of any personal or spiritual agency" (Wax and Wax, 495–96). According to Frazer, magic and science in common postulate a world subject to invariable natural laws, whereas religion postulates a world in which events depend on the whim of spirits. Magic was an attempt to manipulate nature based on an erroneous correlation of cause and effect. The two fallacious "laws" underlying magic were those of "similarity" and of "contact or contagion." The law of similarity supposedly is based on the idea that "likes produces like" and led to what is termed homeopathic, sympathetic, or imitative magic. An example of this would be sticking a probe into the head of a human effigy to give the vicitim a headache. The law of contagion postulates that things once in contact continue to act upon each other, leading to "contagious magic," according to Frazer. Examples would be various machinations over fingernail or hair clippings of an intended victim to produce a desired result. In this manner Frazer isolated what he believed to be the two main types of associations in magic, magic being conceived of, following Tylor, as the misapplication of the association of ideas.

Finally, we come to Bronislaw Malinowski, who was born in Krakow, Poland, in 1884 and died in New Haven, Connecticut, in 1942. Upon receiving his Ph.D. in mathematics from his native city's venerable university in 1908, he began working in chemistry and physics. Like Tylor, he temporarily had to abandon his chosen field of professional endeavor due to ill health, and this led eventually to his lifelong dedication to anthropology. To pass the time, young Bronislaw began reading Frazer's *The Golden Bough*. In his own words, "No sooner had I read this great work than I became immersed in it and enslaved by it" (Hays 1964:314). As his health improved, he went in 1910 to London, where he made the acquaintance of Frazer and was trained in anthropology by A.C. Haddon and C.G. Seligman at the London School of Economics. In 1914 he undertook field research in New Guinea.

As fate would have it, World War I began, and Malinowski became an enemy alien, as officially he was a citizen of the Austro-Hungarian Empire. It was arranged for him to be interned in the Trobriand Islands, where he spent four years. In this fortuitous manner, much to the chagrin of future generations of aspiring young Ph.D. candidates in the discipline, Malinowski set the standards for modern anthropological fieldwork. Malinowski relates how he spent the first year in the islands depressed and reading novels. Then, leaving the company of the Australian traders, he went out to live with the Trobrianders and learn their way of life. In his own words:

> There is all the difference between a sporadic plunging into the company of natives, and being really in contact with them. What does this latter mean? On the Ethnographer's side, it means that his life in the village, which at first is a strange, sometimes unpleasant, sometimes intensely interesting adventure, soon adopts quite a natural course very much in harmony with his surroundings. Soon after I had established myself in Omarakana, I began to take part, in a way, in the village life, to look forward to the important or festive events, to take personal interest in the gossip and the developments of the small village occurrences; to wake up every morning to a day, presenting itself to me more or less as it does to the native. . . . I could see the arrangements for the day's work, people starting on their errands, or groups of men and women busy at some manufacturing tasks. Quarrels, jokes, family scenes, events usually trivial, sometimes dramatic, but always significant, formed the atmosphere of my daily life, as well as of theirs. (Kaberry 1957:78)

Such immersion in the people he studied allowed him to become aware of what he liked to call "the imponderabilia of actual life":

> Here belong such things as the routine of a man's working day; . . . the tone of conversational and social life around the village fires, the existence of strong friendships or hostilities, and of passing sympathies and dislikes between people; the subtle yet unmistakable manner in which personal vanities and ambitions are reflected in the behavior of the individual and in the emotional reactions of those who surround him. . . . Indeed, if we remember that these imponderable yet all-important facts of actual life are part of the real substance of the social fabric, that in them are spun the innumerable threads which keep together the family, the clan, the village community, the tribe — their significance becomes clear. (Kaberry: 78–9)

Returning to London in 1921, Malinowski began teaching and in time was appointed to the first chair in anthropology at the University of London in 1927. In 1938 he settled in the United States and eventually became professor of anthropology at Yale University.

Malinowski has been described as a vibrant personality, intolerant of what he considered to be sham or insincerity, easily slighted and insensitive "to the effects of his exuberance towards others" (Firth 1957:1). My favorite descriptive remark concerning Malinowski is by the famous British social anthropologist, Raymond Firth: "In pubic speaking Malinowski could be most witty, and complimentary or provocative, as he chose. But his gift was not always sure; at times also he could be most laboriously unfunny" (Firth 1957:12).

Among Malinowski's most famous works are *The Family Among the Australian Aborigines* (1913), *Argonauts of the Western Pacific* (1922), *Crime and Custom in Savage Society* (1926), *Sex and Repression in Savage Society* (1927), *The Sexual Life of Savages in Northwestern Melanesia* (1929), *Coral Gardens and Their Magic* (1935), *Freedom and Civilization* (1944), *A Scientific Theory of Culture* (1944), and *The Dynamics of Culture Change* (1945).

Malinowski had intimate, sustained, and systematic knowledge of a small-scale nonliterate society. This experience placed him at a distinct advantage in relation to Tylor and Frazer, who had to rely on the sometimes faulty and unsystematic observations of European explorers, missionaries, administrators, and traders. These latter sources often gave undue attention to what they considered the curious, crude, or sensational. The results of Malinowski's attempt to apply Tylor's and Frazer's ideas to a thorough analysis of one culture are thus particularly revealing. The clearest statement of these results is in Malinowski's classic essay, "Magic, Science and Religion," which originally appeared in a collection of essays, *Science, Religion and Reality* (1925).

Malinowski begins by implicitly reprimanding Tylor and Frazer, stating:

> Magic and religion are not merely a doctrine or a philosophy, not merely an intellectual body of opinion, but a special mode of behavior, a pragmatic attitude built up of reason, feeling, and will alike. It is a mode of action as well as a system of belief, and a sociological phenomenon as well as a personal experience. (1948:24)

He then goes on to correct the prevalent turn-of-the-century caricature of those living in small-scale nonliterate societies. This caricature depicted the so-called primitive mind as "superstitious, childlike, incapable of either critical or sustained thought" (Evans-Pritchard 1965:8). This subsection in Malinowski's work is entitled "Rational Mastery by Man of his Surroundings." Speaking primarily in reaction to the work of Levy-Bruhl, the French philosopher and student of anthropology who had postulated the existence of prelogical primitive mentality, Malinowski asserted that "every primitive community is in possession of a considerable store of knowledge, based on experience and fashioned by reason" (1948:26). He pointed out that the Trobriand Islanders are expert fishermen as well as industrious manufacturers and cultivators.

Having established this point, Malinowski goes on to introduce his concepts of magic and religion into the analysis of Trobriand culture. To appreciate his thinking on these matters, one must first understand his general orientation to what he considered to be the "science of culture." Malinowski believed that culture should be viewed as an instrumentality designed to satisfy needs that were primarily biological and, secondarily and derivatively, social. By uncovering the contemporary relationship between cultural instrumentality and basic human needs, Malinowski believed one was simultaneously uncovering the origins of cultural institutions: "The search for origins thus becomes really an analysis of cultural phenomena in relation, on the one hand, to man's biological endowment, and on the other, to his relationship to the environment" (1944b:203). Such a formula for synchronically uncovering origins is, I believe, at the heart of Malinowski's pronounced tendency to equate his findings for the Trobriand Islanders with definitive statements concerning humankind in general. As will be evident in a moment, he steps back and forth between Trobriand Islanders and humankind and between supposed function and origin with little discomfort.

Malinowski reasons that early man, faced with his inadequate scientific knowledge, rebels against his impotence through magic. He emphasizes the emotional setting, the gestures and expressions of the magician during his performance. Speaking of an example of what Frazer would have termed sympathetic magic, Malinowski states:

The sorcerer has, as an essential part of the ritual performance, not merely to point the bone dart at his victim, but with an intense expression of fury and hatred he has to thrust it in the air, turn and twist it as if to bore it in the wound, then pull it back with a sudden jerk. Thus not only is the act of violence, or stabbing, reproduced, but the passion of violence has to be enacted.

We see thus that the dramatic expression of emotion is the essence of this act, for what is it that is reproduced in it? Not its end, for the magician would in that case have to imitate the death of the victim, but the emotional state of the performer, a state which closely corresponds to the situation in which we find it and which has to be gone through mimetically. (1948:71)

Thus magic, to Malinowski, is derived not from observation of nature or faulty knowledge of its laws, as Tylor and Frazer would have it, but instead springs from situationally induced emotion. The belief in its efficacy must, he reasoned, have arisen from this emotional situation:

And what is the purely intellectual process, the conviction formed during such a free outburst of emotion in words and deeds? First there surges a clear image of the desired end, of the hated person, of the feared danger or ghost. And each image is blended with its specific passion, towards that image. When passion reaches the breaking point at which man loses control over himself, the words which he utters, his blind behavior, allow the pent-up physiological tension to flow over. But over all this outburst presides the image of the end . . . As the tension spends itself in these words and gestures the obsessing visions fade away, the desired end seems nearer satisfaction, we regain our balance, once more at harmony with life . . . In brief, a strong emotional experience, which spends itself in a purely subjective flow of images, words, and acts of behavior, leaves a very deep conviction of its reality, as if of some practical and positive achievement, as if of something done by a power revealed to man. (1948: 80, 81)

Malinowski emphasizes that, for most nonliterate people, magic is not primarily generated from experience, but is an accepted belief in his culture that predates his birth. It is believed to be "a primeval possession of man known only through tradition" (1948:76).

In spite of his different treatment of the origin and nature of magic, Malinowski remained, to some extent, committed to the formula-

tions of Tylor and Frazer.* In a somewhat forced manner, he continued their tradition of viewing magic as a pseudoscience:

> Magic is akin to science in that it always has a definite aim intimately
> associated with human instincts, needs, and pursuits. The magic art is
> directed towards the attainment of practical aims. Like the other arts and
> crafts, it is also governed by a theory, by a system of principles which
> dictate the manner in which the act has to be performed in order to be
> effective. In analyzing magical spells, rites, and substances we have found
> that there are a number of general principles which govern them. Both
> science and magic develop a special technique. (1948:86)

In a manner similar to his treatment of magic, Malinowski views
what he considers to be religion as arising from, and involved in, situations of emotional stress. He notes the ritual handling of the various
highlights in the human life cycle, such as birth, initiation into tribal
mysteries, marriage, and, most important from his perspective, death.
His observations concerning death are the key to his whole treatment
of religion:

> The savage is intensely afraid of death, probably as the result of some
> deep-seated instincts common to man and animals. He does not want
> to realize it as an end, he cannot face the idea of complete cessation, of
> annihilation. The idea of spirit and of spiritual existence is near at hand,
> furnished by such experiences as are discovered and described by Tylor . . .
> In the various ceremonies at death, in commemoration and communion
> with the departed, and worship of ancestral ghosts, religion gives body
> and form to the saving beliefs. (1948:50, 51)

Thus, according to Malinowski, "Both magic and religion open up
escapes from such situations and such impasses as offer no empirical
way out except by ritual and belief into the domain of the supernatural" (1948:87).

Nevertheless, Malinowski clearly distinguishes between the two
in several respects. He maintains that magical rituals are performed
individually, while religious rituals are performed by the group as
a whole. Of greater significance is his assertion that, whereas magic

---

*It should be noted that Malinowski still held to Tylor's and Frazer's view of magic
as involving the association of ideas but added that this association comes about
through emotion (Malinowski 1948:87).

"is always an affirmation of man's power to cause certain definite effects by a definite spell and rite" (1948:88), religious rituals have no ulterior purpose, the objective being achieved in the ritual itself. For example, the Trobriand Islander can tell you the desired end of a magical rite but, as regards a religious ceremonial, he can only state that this is what is done on such occasions. The former is a consequence of self-interest, the latter of tradition. Returning to the treatment of death, it is significant to note that the Trobriand Islanders do not believe that their mortuary rituals restore life. As Malefijt states, "Mourning rituals do not achieve immortality; they express it" (1968:87).

Two significant questions arise from the works of Tylor, Frazer, and Malinowski: (1) What are the implications of their conceptual tradition of magic, science, and religion for the future study of that part of culture we may term the supernatural? And (2) what are the implications of their work for our understanding of our own way of life?

At the beginning of this essay I stated that I regard the conceptual tradition embodied in the works of Tylor, Frazer, and Malinowski as part of the continuing attempt to relate, in a meaningful manner, different ways of life to our own. This is the central challenge to which contemporary anthropology responds. Seen from the perspective of the physical sciences, the theories of Tylor, Frazer, and Malinowski are not scientific theories. However, seen from the perspective of this challenge, viewing anthropology and the social sciences as intimately related to the humanities, these theories appear in a different light.

To Tylor, many of the beliefs of nonliterate peoples were wrong. However, Tylor *was* attempting to show that nonliterate cultures are based on logic and reason no less than our own. Given the limited empirical knowledge of the nonliterates, their inferences, if incorrect, at least are reasonable. While it is true that Frazer picked up and elaborated upon Tylor's view of magic as a form of pseudo-science, his efforts were not devoted to downgrading the peoples he wrote of in his books. Rather he seemed to be attempting to bring them closer to us by emphasizing their similar stance toward life. For example, consider the following quote from *The Golden Bough*:

The analogy between the magical and the scientific conceptions of the world is close. In both of them the succession of events is perfectly regular and certain, being determined by immutable laws, the operation of which can be foreseen and calculated precisely; the elements of caprice, of chance, and of accident are banished from the course of nature. Both of them open up a seemingly boundless vista of possibilities to him who knows the causes of things and can touch the secret springs that set in motion the vast and intricate mechanism of the world. (Wax and Wax 1963:496).

In the same fashion, Malinowski's emphasis on the practical knowledge of nonliterate peoples; his diligent though unsuccessful efforts to indicate the separation between the domains of magic, science, and religion in the minds of the Trobriand Islanders; and his very conceptualization of these domains demonstrate his efforts to provide a meaningful context for our interaction with the cultural other. As E.R. Leach states: "It was dogma for Malinowski that all human beings are reasonable (sensibly practical) individuals. To understand the significance of this belief we need to remember that at the beginning of Malinowski's anthropological career the 'savage' was commonly regarded as a sub-rational human being" (1957:127, 128). This context is the key to the essay "Magic, Science and Religion" and is also reflected in his book on Trobriand law, *Crime and Custom in Savage Society*. In this work Malinowski attempts to demonstrate that nonliterate peoples are not "slaves to custom" who automatically obey rules, but instead are rational, calculating beings like ourselves.

In retrospect, the efforts of all three scholars seem to have fallen far short of their mark. In their writings nonliterate humankind still appears as a somewhat infantile, misguided, and superstitious being. Why? One possibility is that, indeed, humankind in nonliterate cultures is infantile, misguided, and superstitious. I reject such an answer as a figment of our own enculturation. It does not accord with my own experience or those of many gifted anthropologists whose work I respect. However, I would be deceiving you if I made it appear that such rejection is based solely on the empirical evidence. For such a rejection is also an act of anthropological faith. It amounts to saying that what I do not understand about an institution or belief that is clearly meaningful in another culture is a result of *my own* ignorance, not the ignorance of the members of that other culture.

It is from this stance that I have found the engaging problems of anthropology to emerge. Despite their great efforts, Tylor, Frazer, and Malinowski could not come to terms with the nonliterate cultural other, except as an inferior version of themselves. All three were trapped in the dogmas of utilitarianism, progressive cultural development, and intellectualism.

Malinowski, for example, was deeply committed to showing the Trobriand Islanders as "practical," "sensible," "pragmatic," and "reasonable," but always in terms of our culture's understandings of these concepts. He ended by distorting our concepts of science (see Nadel 1957, Wax and Wax 1963) and reason. Ironically, he was forced seriously to distort the Trobrianders' own sense of their culture, as is demonstrated in several excellent essays by Dorothy Lee (1949, 1950) which employ Malinowski's own materials to alter significantly our understanding of Trobriand culture.

It would be unprofitable to enter fully into a discussion of the ethnocentrism of Tylor, Frazer, and Malinowski. Indeed, given their milieu, such a criticism would be unfairly hurled backward in time. However, it is worth remembering that Malinowski was capable of the following statement, which was the concluding paragraph of his essay on magic, science, and religion:

> Looking from far and above, from our high places of safety in developed civilization, it is easy to see all the crudity and irrelevance of magic. But without its power and guidance early man could not have mastered his practical difficulties as he has done, nor could man have advanced to the higher stages of culture. Hence the universal occurrence of magic in primitive societies and its enormous sway. Hence do we find magic an invariable adjunct of all important activities. I think we must see in it the embodiment of the sublime folly of hope, which has yet been the best school of man's character. (1948:90)

Given the untold millions killed in needless warfare and holocausts since that statement was written in 1925, the environmental debacle that surrounds us, the social and political malaise in our society, to many our civilization's place seems no longer so high or so safe as it did to Malinowski, though none of this diminishes its natural need of the sublime.

The tradition made too much of supernatural beliefs, for historical and cultural rather than for theoretical reasons. The great success of supernatural cultural forms and the historical persecution of science by religion both enter into the attempt to explain away supernatural beliefs and their associated behaviors. Such beliefs are both less and more than the scientific mind in the strict sense can understand. The naturalistic mind, in general, is not so limited. It can see both the why of belief and the danger of naivete. While the need is more for sublimation than sublimity if we are to have a natural moral order, it is not necessary simply to dismiss the supernatural as "unscientific" in our mind if not the world. Better to see it as "nonscientific" (dare I say poetic?) and come to terms with it through an attempt to engage in a natural moral dialogue on behalf of us all.

In a series of notes published posthumously as "Remarks on Frazer's *The Golden Bough*," Ludwig Wittgenstein essentially dismissed the line of attack employed by both Fraser and Tylor. The demonstration that religion and magic are not science is a small accomplishment, at best, to Wittgenstein's mind. Indeed, religion rarely makes such claims anymore, "creation science" aside. Perhaps this in part results from the work of Frazer, Tylor, and Malinowski, all of whom viewed magic and religion as wrong. This view may have been a necessary corrective. But their earlier work allows us today to view magic and religion as human acts and creations rendered in the poetic mode and conceived, in the first instance, independently of technology, science, and philosophy. Frazer's naivete lies in his failure to discern the full significance of the distinction between poetry and technology. Like Malinowski, Wittgenstein appreciates the expressivity of supernatural beliefs, their symbolic creativity, far more than Frazer or Tylor. Wittgenstein champions an empathic understanding as the intellectual solution to whatever "problem" their existence poses for the naturally reflective mind.

Fraser and Tylor emphasized the reasonable, if incorrect, origins of magic and religion. Malinowski can be said to have understood them in the humanistic or empathic sense but also to have felt a great obligation to apologize for them. Wittgenstein did neither. He did not see magic as ultimately a pseudotechnical event because it had a goal it could not achieve and was based on untrue—that is, unscientific—beliefs. He appreciated these acts as poetic, symbolic events, as human events. For Wittgenstein, magic "gives a wish a representation; it expresses a wish" (1967:237). To his mind, human "subjectivity" was not to be destroyed in the name of science but rather was to be understood and appreciated through natural inquiry. Wittgenstein's mind was undisturbed by the existence of many views of the human condition. He berates the scientistic mind for always demanding an explanation. Thus, he puts forward a more fully human, rather than simply and exclusively "objective," understanding as the goal of anthropology. Without denying science its fundamental place, Wittgenstein saw that anthropology could be more. The consideration of human affect is at once the most obvious and the most profoundly complex problem confronting such an anthropology. Simply put, Wittgenstein does not equate subjectivity or subjective understanding with error. Rather, he explores the understanding of empathy and the judgment of common humanity.

To Wittgenstein, the fact that we can use categories such as "magic" and "religion" to talk of the cultural other, that we can find comparable dimensions in disparate ways of life, is absolutely amazing and attests to the universal nature and the finite condition of human consciousness. It is the subjectivity of human consciousness, thought with a personal referent, that is the ultimate source of human culture and specifically of human moral concerns. Such subjectivity may not be useful in the physical sciences, but it is fundamental in both the social sciences and the humanities. The possession of science distances us far less from the nonliterate than Malinowski imagined. We and they are faced equally with the central challenge of human consciousness—to discover through pursuit, the good life. However, while neither the possession nor the absence of scientific knowledge is a guarantee of the good life for either the individual or society as a whole, it is my faith as a scientific humanist that such knowledge is an irreplaceable resource. The birth of science simultaneously brought naivete into the human world. Without naivete, there can be no maturity. Yet the scientific mind, in and of itself, is not the mature mind.

If human subjectivity is given a central place in culture theory and in anthropology in general, the natural/supernatural distinction, without being destroyed, can be diminished as a barrier to appreciative understanding. As creatures of human consciousness, we must accept an inevitable degree of isolation. To destroy the distinction is to invite abominations of consciousness such as "creation science." Empathy is reaching out across the boundaries of selfhood. It is a cognitive and affective state of union. It is also a personal state and a temporal one. To breach the barriers of human isolation is not to destroy them. The personal understanding of human subjectivity does not destroy the potential for judgment; rather, it can cultivate it through fostering a greater appreciation of cultural creativity and human diversity. To experience the multitudinous dimensions of human subjectivity, to take them seriously, is a means through which we can nourish and mature our personal appraisals. This is a matter of faith for the cultural relativist. Perhaps, in this manner, supernatural beliefs and practices can be appreciated for the meaningful cultural creativity they exhibit rather than condemned and demeaned for the science they lack. Is the poet to be appreciated less than the physicist?

Wittgenstein said of magic, "An error only arises when magic is interpreted scientifically" (1967:237). He chastised Frazer for the customary nature of his consciousness: "What narrowness of spiritual life in Frazer! Hence: how impossible for him to comprehend a life different from the English life of his time" (1967:237).

Wittgenstein approached supernatural behavior and beliefs through affect and empathy, as did Malinowski. But, whereas Malinowski sought to explain "errors," Wittgenstein sought to recognize a common human condition that informs all customary existences. Thus, his position allows us to see anthropology as self-study through an attempt to understand the human other. Humanistic anthropology seeks to describe the cultural other in terms that are uniquely appropriate to the natural study of human beings among all the phenomena of our existence, by means that include introspection and self-extension.

One can understand empathically because one's experiences permit one to see the point of a matter. Such understanding is not simply the truth of explanation or answer but also the truth of identification, of personal insight. In anthropology, among all of the naturalistic studies, these insights are very important. The doctrine of cultural relativism shifts the emphasis from explanation, in the strict scientific sense of cause and effect, to understanding in the broader humanistic sense of appreciative identification through the translation of the cultural other into the self of common humanity.

Rather than establishing a hierarchy based on the possession of empirical truths, cultural relativism seeks the harmonies of normative expectations through a self-cognizant tolerance. The quest for natural moral being thus takes on the character of a science of limits, as Philip Rieff (1972) would have it. For natural moral discourse begins with the consideration of the natural moral limits of human empathic understanding.

From the perspective of scientific humanism, the historical anthropological tradition under consideration is instructive precisely as it moves from viewing the other, in this case "magic" and "religion," as inferior versions of self, in this case "science," and begins to translate them into our own affective existence. Both the catharsis of magic and the saving beliefs of religion speak to affective needs that cannot be banished as the scientist would banish "subjectivity." Subjectivity speaks to human need far more than it does to human error. Is the feeling that one is a decent person, a desirable person, a "mensch," to be tested by science in the name of natural truth? If so, on what basis? What precisely is the relationship between science and the affective needs of human beings? Scientific humanism is in part an attempt to address such issues. Freud observed that natural truth is all the truth we have as human beings. This does not make it, in and of itself, sufficient. Thus we must explore rather than deny the relationship between "is" and "ought" in our search for valued direction. We must make the contemporary mythic movement (see "The Contextual Background" in chapter 1 above).

In religion, the need is to contract claims and ambitions in the contemporary world, while in science, the need is to expand the cultural significance of its endeavors. The scientists need deeply to acknowledge their personal responsibility for their activities in the world. Truth may be ethically neutral, but as the twentieth century has taught, the human uses of truth are not. Scientific humanism seeks to build this moral dimension of science by seeing science itself as expressive of a world view, as possessed of values that constitute a vision of a human way of life, a genuinely cultural way of being. As Jacob Bronowski observed, "There are some traditional values alive in our scientific society today; but whether they are traditional or whether they are new, they are alive not by accident, but because they are appropriate: because they fit into, and grow from, the activity of science. It is time that those who discuss values learn the reach of that activity and the power of the values which spring from its modest search, personal and communal at the same time, for the factual truth" (1977:220)

Scientific humanism is not a religion, for it involves no supernatural beliefs. But the values of science do express a faith, a faith in an integrated common humanity and human reason as a spiritual force in the contemporary life of the mind. It is this faith that underlies the potential of science for the constitution of natural moral systems. Human needs and affective concerns are not simply explanatory elements that allow us to dismiss supernatural beliefs as untrue. They are also major dimensions of the existential challenges to meaningful being that allow us to appreciate the artistry of the supernatural as a human and often a humane creation. The tradition of magic, science, and religion, by its very juxtaposition of concepts, deprecates this artistry, its angle of comparison and translation; is ethnocentric; and, in terms of culture theory, is no longer central to the contemporary thrust of the anthropology of religion. Robert Bellah has said of science and religion, "They have different purposes, different limitations, different modes of action. But they are both part, and I would argue a necessary part, of every culture and every person. They need to exist in some vital and healthy whole in which each is integral" (1970:244).

Surely, in this post-Holocaust world of moral failure, we can mature and foster our understandings and judgments regarding the coexistence and proper relationships of science and religion. To see them at this point in time simply as sequential stages of human intellectual maturity is silly. Yet, as a scientific humanist, I must testify to my conviction that the truths of science must be honored with more, not less, certainty than we would grant the truths of not only Jerry Falwell or Jimmy Swaggart, but of our more highly respected religious functionaries as well. The very tentativeness, yet usefulness, of scientific knowledge gives it impressive claims to appropriately describing the reality in which we live as human beings. The earliest humanists believed that we could not arrive at the good or the beautiful without first acknowledging the ascendancy of the true and its finite domains. It is not by chance that very few scientists, in their professional capacities, are fanatics, charlatans, or self-aggrandizing egoists.

While science plays a fundamental role in our culture, the scientific conception of human subjectivity cannot be allowed to dominate our thinking about human consciousness and the human condition. The foundation of a significant scientific humanism is not simply Western science, but must be, more generally, existential mystery of the kind expressed in the first four lines of Lao Tzu's Tao Te Ching:

> The way that can be told
> Is not the constant way;
> The name that can be named
> Is not the constant name. (1963:57)

We must come to see the existential mystery that surrounds natural moral being and constitutes the backdrop against which we seek to make natural moral sense.

Both natural and supernatural disciplines can accept existential mystery as their foundation. It is the common human reality. Religion must abandon its absolutist tendencies, while science must abandon its illusions of self-sufficiency and insulation if an appropriate relationship between "is" and "ought" is to be realized. We all know much less than we think we do.

The concept of culture that emerges from such a grounding is stimulating and fruitful. Culture no longer appears as an epiphenomenal creation superimposed on a preexistent reality; rather, it is the meaningful human reality, the stance toward life, brought about by the traditional, social manipulation of symbols and experience in relation to the responses of a particular individual in question. It is the synthesis of humankind's social nature and individual consciousness. We live, not only as collectivities, but as individuals, in cultural realities. The central question that emerges from such a conceptualization is not which collective or individual culture is higher or lower, more advanced or backward, superior or inferior, but rather to what extent a society and its individuals have, and are continuing to maintain, the cultural resources necessary for the constitution of meaningful cultural realities. As Ruth Benedict observed, "In reality, society and the individual are not antagonists. His culture provides the raw material of which the individual makes his life. If it is meager, the individual suffers; if it is rich, the individual has the chance to rise to his opportunity" (1959:252).

Speaking of anthropology, the gifted practitioner Marshall Sahlins observed: "Modern civilization knows no borders: those curious peoples beyond the pale have been drawn into the main stream in the course of Europe's four century planetary reconnaissance. Once discovered, they were rapidly colonized, baptized, and culturally traumatized—'acculturated' is the technical term. . . . And now, having bit deeply into native custom, civilization allows itself the luxury of an intellectual digestion" (1968:1). We may well have destroyed the souls of the many fragile cultural creations of nonliterate humanity, like the proverbial bull in the china shop. Nevertheless, the fact remains that we have their bodies. Thus, for their sake, as well as for ours, the self-conscious and emotionally mature perspectives and attitudes that flow from appreciative interaction with the cultural other must be attained. It is as if a great pendulum has swung, and once again we must collectively, yet as individuals, meet the primitive challenge of creating humanly meaningful and mutually supportive realities. Here's hoping we do so in the spirit of my older son, David, who upon seeing his younger brother get into the bathtub before him, a grievous affront, uttered those immortal words: "Joshua and I will both be first. All right, Dad?"

5 The Meaning of "Religion as a Cultural System"

When Buddha was in Grdhrakuta mountain, he turned a flower in his finger and held it before his listeners. Everyone was silent. Only Maha-kashapa smiled at this revelation, although he tried to control the lines of his face. Buddha said:

> I have the eye of the true teaching, the heart of Nirvana, the true aspect of nonform, and the ineffable stride of Dharma. It is not expressed by words, but especially transmitted beyond teaching. This teaching I have given to Maha-Kashapa.

Buddha Twirls a Flower (Reps 1959:95)

He who knows does not say; he who says does not know.

Lao Tzu

I

When future generations of anthropologists set out to rediscover their tradition, the writings of Clifford Geertz will be there to guide the worthy pilgrims (Rice 1980; Shankman 1984). While still in mid-career, Geertz already has achieved a major refocusing of post–World War II anthropology that will connect anthropologists of the last half of the twentieth century to those new endeavors now only dimly perceived on the horizon. His vision of an interpretive theory of culture is as fundamental a contribution as was Emile Durkheim's view of a science of sociology. Nowhere are this relationship and its significance to be seen as clearly as in the "anthropology of religion." If there is an important truth in the characterization of Durkheim's position as "religion is society," then this same truth is contained in the characterization of Geertz's position as "religion is humanity." In the

hope of contributing to the appreciation of Geertz's creation and par-
ticipating in the discussion he seeks to sustain (1973a:29), I offer this
brief discussion of the meaning of his essay, "Religion as a Cultural
System."

Before setting out to ascertain the meaning of Geertz's anthropology of religion, I need to indicate how I here use the words "culture"
and "meaning" in my discussion of "religion." I employ the term
"culture" precisely in the sense explored by Roy Wagner in his wonderful book, *The Invention of Culture*:

> Anthropology is the study of man "as if" there were culture. It is brought
> into being by the invention of culture, both in the general sense, as a con-
> cept, and in the specific sense, through the invention of particular cul-
> tures. Since anthropology exists through the idea of culture, this has
> become its overall idiom, a way of talking about, understanding, and
> dealing with things, and it is incidental to ask whether cultures exist.
> They exist through the fact of their being invented, and through the effec-
> tiveness of this invention. This invention need not take place in the course
> of field-work; it can be said to occur whenever and wherever some "alien"
> or "foreign" set of conventions is brought into relation with one's own. . . .
> This invention, in turn, is part of the more general phenomenon of hu-
> man creativity—it transforms the mere assumption of culture into a cre-
> ative art. (1975:10–11)

For the issue at hand, one of the implications of Wagner's astute observations is that when Geertz speaks of "religion," he is speaking
of an "alien" set of conventions. I wish to explore what about religion is alien to Geertz. Within his presentation is an implicit comparison of religion and anthropology as "particular manners of con-
struing the world" (1973c:110). Can one doubt that the dominant
way Geertz construes human existence is through anthropology?
Thus, whatever else his anthropology of religion is, it must be a focusing on the distinction between religion and anthropology.

The meaning, the intellectual significance, of Clifford Geertz's
essay, "Religion as a Cultural System," is its intention (Grice 1971:
442). Geertz himself has noted that "models of" simultaneously function as "models for." Thus, to inquire into the implicit intention
embedded in his model of religion is to seek to uncover the model
"for" religion it assuredly contains.

Meaning as intention focuses on the human creator and in so doing allows us to treat the literature of social science with an appropriate sensitivity to the question of the fiction of science. Geertz has written of science as a "genre of cultural expression" (1975:26). The hallmark of this genre is the acknowledged attempt on the part of the scientist to create a symbol system that, in a highly significant and paradoxical way, simultaneously denies the creativity of the scientist involved in the endeavor. "Objectivity," the masterful achievement of the fiction of science, can be appreciated with facility in "social science," that extension of the scientific art into the area of social studies. This uniquely contemporary genre of human discourse demands an artistry that can revise the painfully familiar by appearing to remove the humanity from its rendition.

In its anthropological guise, the genre of science achieves truth through self-parody, as it employs the vocabulary of objectivity to assert the humanity of the strange to an unacknowledged audience of the familiar. Thus, in the translation of an exotic culture into anthropological categories for the anonymous reader, not only can the devotee read the author into the descriptive text, but also, in time, the text itself undergoes an exciting metamorphosis from a window onto the strange into a strange mirror, which more than simply reflects the familiar.

No adept of this slight of reason known as anthropology is more aware of this metamorphosis than Clifford Geertz. Geertz roots his discourse in the lessons of our anthropological past and in the realization that our professional past is only a microcosm of the human past. As Melville Herskovits (1955) sought to clarify in his doctrine of culture relativism, world history is an uncomplimentary reflection of its leading protagonists. The history of the Euro-American cultural world is a tragic testimony to the pronounced tendency of the individual and the group to express, often at the expense of others, their respective biographical and social experience. The judgments of others, and the very real consequences of actions facilitated by those judgments, powerfully reflected the unsuspected nature of the familiar Western culture. While our predecessors were struck by the supposed bizarre differences, the deficiencies of the superstititous primitives, today our view of the "nonprogressives," "nonmoderns," "non-Westerners" has matured. With that maturation has come a revisioning of our immediate intellectual predecessors. Precisely at this juncture Geertz enters professional discourse with the voice of a more fully self-cognizant Durkheim and speaks as the anthropological quester for meaning. In this light we can fruitfully approach the creation of culture thus far achieved by Geertz in his semiotic vision of anthropology as "interpretive science," and his "anthropology of religion." Simply stated, Geertz is attempting a science of human creativity, a science of culture, a science of fiction, while simultaneously keeping us fully aware of the fiction of science.

By a science of fiction, I do not mean to oppose culture to fact, but to indicate the necessity of a creative movement beyond the facts — what I term "the mythic movement" (1977). This movement, or cultivation of humanity, is not a leap into fantasy but rather a painful struggle within the reality of our own existence, to achieve a disciplined form, consciously to cultivate a creative partiality that manifests in a concrete, objective way the intangible truth of our existence. So conceived, a science of fiction investigates the lived truths of humanity. Geertz, through his concept of the cultural system, is working toward a theory of culture. Such a theory by definition must be metacultural and grounded in the context of a reality beyond its own creation, in terms of which it can be objectively read.

II
As we seek to ascertain Geertz's intention in "Religion as a Cultural System," E.E. Evans-Pritchard can be of assistance. In the introduction to his somewhat tongue-in-cheek survey of "theories of primitive religion as science," he observes:

> It was rare indeed that those scholars who set themselves up as authorities on primitive religion showed in their interpretations that they had more than a superficial understanding of the historical religions and of what the ordinary worshipper in them believes, what meaning what he does has for him, and how he feels when he does it. (1965:17)

Evans-Pritchard, then, showing great ingenuity and setting the stage for the remainder of his book, asserts:

> What I have said does not imply that the anthropologist has to have a religion of his own, and I think we should be clear on this point at the outset. He is not concerned, qua anthropologist, with the truth or falsity

of religious thought. As I understand this matter, there is no possibility of his knowing whether the spiritual beings of primitive religions or of any others have any existence or not, and since that is the case he cannot take the question into consideration. The beliefs are for him sociological facts, not theological facts, and his sole concern is with their relation to each other and to other social facts. His problems are scientific, not metaphysical or ontological. The method he employs is that now often called the phenomenological one—a comparative study of beliefs and rites, such as God, sacrament, and sacrifice, to determine their meaning and social significance. The validity of the belief lies in the domain of what may broadly be designated the philosophy of religion. It was precisely because so many anthropological writers did take up a theological position, albeit a negative and implicit one, that they felt that an explanation of primitive religious phenomena in causal terms was required, going, it seems to me, beyond the legitimate bounds of the subject. (1965:17).

I suspect that Evans-Pritchard was not aware of a close relationship between the "phenomenological method" and positive theology. Indeed, it was negative theology and its obsession with reductive causation that he sought to reveal as vulnerable. While Geertz probably would be uncomfortable with such a phrasing, his writings on religion express a contemporary positive theology, albeit an implicit one.*

I wish to explicate Geertz's position precisely, because, rather than being a transgression of the "legitimate bounds of the subject," it is, I believe, at the heart of anthropology as a contemporary discipline. For anthropology's role in the modern life of the mind is to involve itself in dialogue with other disciplines, as much as it is to pursue basic research. As I read and reread Geertz's writings on religion, it becomes increasingly difficult for me to maintain the illusions that

---

*In regard to Geertz, I am not using the term "theology" in its traditional religious meaning, but rather as an extension of Philip Rieff's sterling contribution to the theoretical enterprise, and particularly his concept of dogma: "By Dogma I mean a temporarily authoritative consensus of received interpretations, workings-through of some doctrine, toward conduct rationalized in doctrinal terms. Dogma implies not only authority, but resistance to authority. Without heresy, there would have been no dogma. Without resistance, there can be no truth. . . . Every dogma has its term, or terms, without which nothing greatly significant can be conceived to follow; these I call god-terms. . . . All dogmas, including those expressing the authority of science, are mortal codes of immortal commands" (Rieff 1979:358–59). Can anyone doubt that the dominant god-term of American anthropology is culture?

"beliefs are for him sociological facts" and that his sole concern is "with their relation to each other and to other social facts."

To the mind of Geertz, religious thinkers must acknowledge the interpretive nature of their endeavor, and, of course, culture theorists must do likewise. Speaking of theory, Geertz has written:

> The besetting sin of interpretive approaches to anything—literature, dreams, symptoms, culture—is that they tend to resist, or to be permitted to resist, conceptual articulation and thus to escape systematic modes of assessment. . . . For a field of study which, however timidly (though I myself am not timid about the matter at all), asserts itself to be a science, this just will not do. There is no reason why the conceptual structure of a cultural interpretation should be any less formulable, and thus less susceptible to explicit canons of appraisal, than that of, say, a biological observation or a physical experiment—no reason except that the terms in which such formulations can be cast are, if not wholly nonexistent, very nearly so. We are reduced to insinuating theories because we lack the power to state them. (1973a:24)

While I admire Geertz's quest for, and attainment of, clarity, I do not see this as the primary value of his anthropology of religion. This clarity is a secondary component, a personal style of anthropological discourse, put to good use but certainly not the meaning of his accomplishment. Geertz's emulation and indeed exemplification of the scientific posturing of anthropology contains considerable irony, which the serious reader will appreciate. The irony is utilized to highlight the creation of meanings, the movement beyond the facts, the mythmakings that are Geetz's true attainment. Contrary to his contention, there is one good reason why the conceptual structure of a cultural interpretation, if no less formulable than a biological observation or a physical experiment, is less susceptible to explicit canons of appraisal. The reason, as Geertz is well aware, lies in the creative nature of human beings. The point in the case of Geertz, is not that self-conscious human beings can become aware of the predictions of the cultural scientist and, through a Kantian effort of free will, alter their previous pattern of behavior. For Geertz has enunciated as his second condition of cultural theory that "it is not, at least in the strict meaning of the term, predictive" (1973:26). Nor is the issue simply, as Edward Sapir, following Heinrich Rickert, felt, a distinction between historical science and natural science, wherein the former "differs from natural science, either wholly or as regards relative emphasis, in its adherence to the real world of phenomena, not, like the latter, to the simplified and abstract world of ideal concepts" (Sapir 1917:446). For, while historical science "strives to value the unique or individual, not the universal" (Sapir 1917:446), Geertz has argued that "the essential task of theory building here is not to codify abstract regularities but to make thick descriptions possible, not to generalize across cases but to generalize within them" (Geertz 1973a:26). Rather, the dilemma that Geertz presents is that, in his scientific rendering of the products of human being independent of their human makers, he has created a lifeless formal phantasm of religious life. It is as if he has offered us a grammar of religion as a cultural system and passed it off as a rhetoric. If read literally, his scientific claims appear to mistake form for substance, vehicle for destination, representation for lived experience. In my view, however, Geertz's cultural science is not simply to be read literally, it is to be read mythically as well. It is a particular representation of the facts that will enable us to move beyond them. His description of the life of art may well apply to the anthropological life itself:

> It is not a plea . . . for the neglect of form, but for seeking the roots of form not in some updated version of faculty psychology but in what I have called elsewhere "the social history of the imagination"—that is, in the construction and deconstruction of symbolic systems as individuals and groups of individuals try to make sense of the profusion of things that happen to them. (1976:1498)

Geetz's representation of religion from the point of view of science is not designed to reduce religion to science, as, for example, Anthony Wallace intended in his book, *Religion: An Anthropological Approach* (1966). Geertz seeks simultaneously to highlight the strengths and weaknesses of both creative endeavors so as to enable a fuller realization of their creative potential.

"The scientific study of myth, and its twin, the mythic study of science, may truly be the infant gods of a new age of long awaited human maturity" (Wilk, 1980). Geertz has given us a scientific study of myth which simultaneously points to the myth of social science: that the investigation of nature is isomorphic with the investigation of humanity. In its anthropological phrasing, the scientific myth seeks to obscure the human creativy, the freedom, at the heart of the cultural conceptualization of human being. Thus, anthropology, if it is to assist in the living of a human life, must be an interpretive science. Anthropology must seek to ascertain the facts of human existence and then cautiously and consciously move beyond those facts to the mythic realm of meaning. To those who would maintain that an "interpretive science" is a contradiction in terms, Geertz can answer in chorus with epistemologists and religionists that scientific fact, in that it is not presuppositionless and that it transforms associations into causes, is at its base mythic. To those who would say that scientific theory should not constitute human meanings, Geertz can answer that this constitution is an essential aspect of realizing the interpretive nature of culture theory. Moreover, the anthropologist should strive to make the interpretive nature of his thought explicit. Culture theory must face the challenge of presenting the human significance of anthropology and dare to make the mythic movement to meaning. This mythic movement is beyond, not in opposition to, the world of facts; no contemporary myth can compel the mature mind to oppose facts. We must seek the cultural through the factual and offer metacultural analysis, interpretations of interpretations, creations based on the respect for human creativity. In this way the Western anthropologist can both make peace with the transcultural claims of the science and establish a dialogue while remaining true to the universal creativity which is the cultural thrust of the discipline.

III

At the conclusion of *The Theories of Primitive Religion*, E.E. Evans-Pritchard makes the following curious observation:

> As far as a study of religion as a factor in social life is concerned, it may make little difference whether the anthropologist is a theist or an atheist, since in either case he can only take into account what he can observe. But if either attempts to go further than this, each must pursue a different path. The nonbeliever seeks some theory—biological, psychological, or sociological—which will explain the illusion; the believer seeks rather to understand the manner in which a people conceives a reality and their relation to it. For both, religion is part of social life, but for the believer it has also another dimension. (Evans-Pritchard 1965:121)

As a first approximation of this other, personal dimension, let me simply state that the reality referred to by Evans-Pritchard is the existence of a world that by definition exceeds the human ability to experience through comprehension. To put it in anthropocentric terms, it is the reality of human beings as finite manifestations. If this is a reality of religion, then the dimension available to the "theist" is the dimension of creative relationship. For human beings to be a part of this world involves the human creation of relationship with this world. One must reach out, extend oneself, to touch that which is beyond one's present grasp. In the Jewish idiom, it is the covenant; in the Bambuti, it is the *molimo*; in the Cheyenne, the world renewal ceremony; but in every case, the vehicle is secondary to the destination. As Geertz in "Religion as a Cultural System" is fully aware, the medium of human relationship is meaning, and this medium is self-contained, in the sense of being self-creating, self-fulfilling, self-justifying, self-evident . . . and ultimately self-transcending. The truth of religion as a cultural system is that, in the pursuit of meaning, we discover and recover relationship. The truth of "Religion as a Cultural System" is that human meaning is not discovered as much as it is created; it is not complete as much as it is eternally in the making. Evans-Pritchard astutely characterized Emile Durkheim's overt position in the following way:

> If Durkheim's theory of religion is true, obviously no one is going to accept religious beliefs any more; and yet, on his own showing, they are generated by the action of social life itself, and are necessary for its persistence. This puts him on the horns of a dilemma, and all he could say to get off them was that, while religion in the spiritual sense is doomed, a secular assembly may produce ideas and sentiments which have the same function. . . . He hoped and expected, like Saint Simon and Comte, that as spiritual religion declined, a secularistic religion of a humanist kind would take its place. (Evans-Pritchard 1965:63–64)

As Evans-Pritchard no doubt understood, such a characterization, however, was untrue to the meaning of Durkheim's religious writings. For the "sacred" is the reality of contrast, the embodiment of the essence of difference and thus of choice, change, and, ultimately, human creativity. Speaking of the diversity of distinctions to be found in the world, the variety of sacred/profane manifestations, Durkheim noted, "Howsoever much the forms of the contrast may vary, the fact of the contrast is universal" (1915:54). He added in a footnote:

> The conception according to which the profane is opposed to the sacred, just as the irrational is to the rational, or the intelligible is to the mysterious, is only one of the forms under which this opposition is expressed. Science being once constituted, it has taken a profane character, especially in the eyes of the Christian religions; from that it appears as though it could not be applied to sacred things. (1915:54)

Durkheim realized that a sacred science, a scientific humanism, is precisely the need of contemporary humanity and that such a science must be interpretive. Geertz, with more of the twentieth century to guide him, realizes that the interpretive nature of social science must be emphasized rather than hidden. Scientific humanism is a mythic science, a science of creative responsibility, a science of human choice. As such a movement beyond the facts, as such a sacred science, scientific humanism in anthropology must remain forever tentative, open to factual revelations from which the journey of recovery must proceed. Thus Geertz's paradoxical intent in his essay on religion is to urge a greater openness to human experience. It is not religion's fictive nature that troubles him, for all cultural life is creative. Rather, it is that, as presently understood, religious systems constitute meanings prior to, and I think in spite of, experience. What makes Geertz uneasy is "the priority of the acceptance of an authoritative criterion in religious matters over the revelation which is conceived to flow from that acceptance" (1973c:110). It is as if he wishes to tell us that we must be careful not to humanize the world beyond a receptivity to human experience, for to do so is to bite our own tail.

According to Geertz, "The basic axiom underlying what we may perhaps call 'the religious perspective' is everywhere the same; he who would know must first believe" (1973c:110). Geertz, like Durkheim before him, wishes to establish the humane interpretive science, by standing that truth on its head: "He who would believe must first know." It is by seeking a complementary relationship, a balance, between these irreducible mirror images of truth, that contemporary humanity may regain its sense of the moral life in society. The discourse between anthropology and religion ultimately is a discourse concerning the nature and proper role of faith in contemporary human inquiry and contemporary human life. Durkheim's message was not that religions are humanly made, but rather that human existence is a sacred making, that human existence is a sacralization of experience through selection and choice constitutive of meaning.

IV

The religious writings of Clifford Geertz constitute a message of heroic striving in the context of a sacred tolerance, a hymn to tentativeness in the tonality of humility. As Geertz deconstitutes religion, he emerges as a shamanic hero, a maker of meanings. Through his tolerant understanding built upon humility before the facts, we in turn recognize respect for self and others as a heroic feeling.

The image of, and the feeling for, the sacred scientist as hero evoked by contemplation of the writings of Clifford Geertz brings to my mind a contemporary shamanic image broad enough to enfold anthropologist and theologian in its human embrace. It is the scene of Jacob Bronowski standing in the pond of Auschwitz prison camp grasping the mud of annihilated humans in his palm and lifting up his voice:

> It is said that science will dehumanize people and turn them into numbers. That is false, tragically false. Look for yourself. This is the concentration camp and crematorium at Auschwitz. This is where people were turned into numbers. Into this pond were flushed the ashes of some four million people. And that was not done by gas. It was done by arrogance. It was done by dogma. It was done by ignorance. When people believe that they have absolute knowledge, with no test in reality, this is how they behave. . . . Every judgement in science stands on the edge of error, and is personal. Science is a tribute to what we can know, although we are fallible. In the end the words were said by Oliver Cromwell: "I beseech you, in the bowels of Christ, think it possible you may be mistaken". . . . We have to cure ourselves of the itch for absolute knowledge and power. We have to close the distance between the push-button order and the human act. We have to touch people. (1973:374)

6   Shamanism and the Cultural Thought of Edward Sapir

Human beings as a life form experience their existence. By nature, they attempt to consciously experience significant aspects of that existence and to make sense of their conscious experience through the creative application of symbolics. The symbolics that human beings find most valuable in making sense, whether through individual and/or mutual efforts, are relatively speaking the symbolics they find to be most meaningful. Therefore, human beings seek to experience their existence in terms of the symbolics they find to be most meaningful. Anthropologists are human beings.

Culture is symbolically mediated experience. It is human experience in its qualitatively human dimensions. The anthropologist is no less a cultural animal than are the other human beings he "investigates." In the last analysis this is the meaning of anthropology and the beginning of the anthropology of meaning.

Stan Wilk "A Perspective on Culture"

The genuine culture is internal, it works from the individual to ends.

Edward Sapir (1924)

A language is to its speaker as a cultural tradition is to its devotee, it provides a symbolic context within which a human being can make sense.

Stan Wilk, "A Metaphor"

In many of the nonliterate societies traditionally studied by anthropologists, a strange religious specialist was found to exist. The anthropologist has called this figure the "shaman," and some scholars have viewed shamanism as the origin of what we call religion. The shaman's calling is announced by a profound crisis involving visions and illness. With the guidance of established shamans, the initiate constitutes a stable relationship with the nonordinary reality he or she experiences in the calling. The shaman becomes the self-healed curer in lifelong contact with nonordinary reality, an experiential dimension of shamanic existence that is not shared with most fellow community members. Shamans can use their knowledge for a variety of ends, often including curing. Thus Ian Robertson defines shamanism as "a belief in the power of medicine men, sorcerers or other specialists in the manipulation of spiritual forces for human ends" [1976:350].

Until the publication of a series of highly successful books by Carlos Castaneda concerning his pursuit of shamanic knowledge, shamanism was little understood and little valued in our culture. It seemed at least to be nonsense, at worst to be the machinations of charlatans and psychotics. The initial four volumes written by Castaneda contain an account of his apprenticeship to an Indian of Yaqui background named Don Juan. He has recounted his subsequent adventures in an additional series of books.

In 1973 Carlos Castaneda received his Ph.D. from the University of California at Los Angeles for his third book, *Journey to Ixtlan*. With his increasing popularity came increasing criticism both within and outside of anthropology [see Beals 1978 and Demille 1976, 1980]. The accuracy and factuality of Castaneda's accounts, as well as the very existence of Don Juan, were called into question.

I shall focus on Castaneda's first four books, recounting his apprenticeship cycle with Don Juan. It is important to remember that the very idea of taking shamanic initiation seriously is absurd to many, and that rendering it meaningful is a substantial part of Castaneda's contribution. Thus, if we were to view Castaneda's work as literature rather than ethnography, we would still be able to appreciate its significance for the development of anthropology. To my mind this appreciation is best accomplished by seeing it in relation to the work of Edward Sapir.

Substantial aspects of Edward Sapir's most insightful thinking on culture are artfully illustrated by the Don Juan books (for example, see Sapir 1917, 1924). The tetralogy can be read as an exploration of territory that Sapir clearly saw on the horizon. Sapir advocated, and Castaneda illustrated, the following anthropological emphases, among others: taking culture to the level of the individual, incorporating the concrete human being into our anthropological discourse, emphasizing the experiential dimensions of human existence, focusing on the therapeutic and creative dimensions of cultural dynamics. To ignore the Don Juan books, as we have largely ignored Sapir's programmatic writings, displays a stubborn — and, I'm afraid, costly — resistance to professional reflectivity.

The apprenticeship legitimately can be interpreted as an archetypal initiatory account. It is a detailed depiction of what John Berryman has termed "the conversion of a child into a person" (1976:93). Thus the apprenticeship points towards a universal dynamic and toward a commonality that is both species-specific and cultural in the generic sense. It depicts the conscious quest for both a sense of self and an affirmative vision of the human life-world, experienced in their necessary unity. To view the tetralogy in the context of a conceptualization of culture that is group-defining in anything less than a species-specific sense runs the risk of turning vital insight into trivia. If we treat human tragedy as if it were a problem in mathematics to which there is one explicitly specifiable and provable answer, we risk seeing anthropological wisdom elude our grasp. I believe that Edward Sapir was keenly aware of this possibility and that his writings profoundly explored a concept of culture that allows us to appreciate the teachings of Don Juan in an anthropologically mature way. Moreover, I believe that the anthropological sense of personal meaning that Sapir sought to explicate in his programmatic writings is highly applicable to the contemporary human context. Specifically, I would characterize Sapir's interests in culture theory as rooted in a vision of a teaching anthropology concerned with the refinement of taste.

Edward Sapir realized that studies in human refinement must be studies in "personal," "concrete," "individual" refinement. Such studies can only address humanity in general by working through particular registrations in individual human lives. Sapir knew that effectively to investigate the lowest common denominators of human existence, an oblique approach that simultaneously addressed the highest common denominators was required. He sensed that the search for a universal humanity, rather than being a naive hope of an infant discipline, was the very soul of anthropology. He believed that, by undertaking the arduous study necessary to refine our appreciation of the human being, we could prepare ourselves professionally to work through manifest particularities in their complex experienced actualities so as to read the deeper, latent universals of the human dynamics. Sapir realized, as does Geertz (1973b) after him, that a mature anthropological discipline must be an interpretive endeavor. But while Geertz thus far has confined his cultural analysis to manifestations on the group level, Sapir realized the rich anthropological possibilities of interpretive cultural analysis at the level of the individual as well.

In his famous exchange with Kroeber regarding the latter's ideas on culture as "superorganic," Sapir, long before his late programmatic essays, maintained that the unity of anthropology as an historical discipline is its investigation of the unique (Sapir 1917:446). He realized that the engaged contemplation of the thin surface of unique manifestations was the surest road to extremely worthwhile anthropological distinctions, such as those between spurious and genuine cultures and between the scientific analysis of individual personality and the humanistic discernment of character and common humanity. Sapir, like many before and after him, shared a secret of wisdom, the realization that to undertake studies having as their goal the refinement of human judgment, one must commit oneself to a value discourse, a mythic or moral discourse that of necessity appears oblique and personal. Refinement is a delicate and complex matter of balancing, one that can be communicated only partially from individual to individual, and then only through seeming indirection. As Lao Tzu eloquently addressed the matter:

> Hence always rid yourself of desires
> in order to observe its secrets;
> But always allow yourself to have desires
> in order to observe its manifestations.
> These two are the same
> But diverge in name as they issue forth.
> Being the same they are called mysteries,
> Mystery upon mystery
> The gateway of the manifold secrets. (1963:57)

Castaneda's contribution to cultural anthropology is most fruitfully assessed in relation to the subfield of symbolic anthropology
(Schneider, Dolgin, and Kemnitzer 1977:84). The vitality of the Don
Juan books derives to a considerable extent from the concrete and
sophisticated presentation of the human being. Rather than "holding the human being constant" so as to reveal the "culture," as Kroeber
or Leslie White (1959) was prone to do, Castaneda allows a flesh-
and-blood protagonist to emerge as the central figure in his atypical
study. Indeed, the tetralogy plays cultural realities off against one
another so as to highlight human being in the modern world (Castaneda 1972:299–302). Should this not be of interest to the contemporary anthropologist faced with the heterogeneity of modern civilizations, a heterogeneity we have yet to address in a conceptually
mature manner? (see Kroeber 1952:150.) I cannot fault Castaneda for
failing to employ the curious anthropological algebra that cancels
out the subtle humanity of the individuals being described. Rather
I applaud his willingness to incorporate his own individuality into
the study. In the apprenticeship cycle, human beings are portrayed
as complex and powerful, self-directing and self-generating. Universal rather than culturally specific human capacities and needs are
brought forward in the bold relief provided by intercultural exchange.
The tetralogy highlights the possibilities of human maturity, transcendence, and synthesis. Here is a vantage point from which to appreciate Castaneda's account of shamanic apprenticeship.

Human life as constituted through symbolic forms is the major
focus of symbolic anthropology. In their potentially, symbolics can
help to unite thought, action, and feeling, human reflection and experience, into a satisfying sense of personal existence. The human
condition is aproached through human consciousness and freedom
(see Schneider, Dolgin, and Kemnitzer 1977:44). Flowing from this
perspective is a tendency to see human being as requiring, at the least,
order, and, more fully, a life-embracing affirmation. Castaneda's work
demonstrates how a serious consideration of Sapir's (1963a) thinking
can provide a vital complement to Geertz's approach to religion and
thereby deepen the potential of symbolic understanding. While I do
not wish to undertake a full discussion of the differing emphases of
Sapir and Geertz, it is important to note several significant contrasts.
Geertz is interested primarily in the symbolic enablement of collec-

tive existence, rather than in the dynamic interplay between human being and cultural setting. His thinking tends to emphasize the cognitive rather than the affective, objectivity rather than human awareness, the constraints of human existence rather than its indeterminant creative possibilities. To overstate a critical difference between these two gifted anthropologists, I would suggest that Geertz's professional efforts tend to locate human creativity, if not human freedom, in collective traditions constituted in the past, while Sapir tended to emphasize the ongoing creative endeavor that the life of an actual human being manifests. Geertz's essay on religion is heavily imbued with the image of culture as traditional mold of the group rather than as contemporary context and medium for the individual.

As a result of this emphasis, the import of Geertz's anthropological insight into religion, like that of Durkheim (1915) before him, is ironic in its consequences. While his own analysis reveals the therapeutic dynamics that can result from a creatively choreographed dance of symbol and experience, the very impact of his culture-consciousness seems to locate these therapeutic dynamics in a past that is lost to us. For Geertz the therapeutic function is dependent on a transaction in believability that his own analysis renders impotent. For his own part, Geertz states that his "aim is not therapy but the analysis of social discourse" (1973a:26). One may legitimately ask, however, "To what end?" In doing so, we realize that Geertz is sidestepping the issue. His disavowal does not remove the fact that his own professional posture exhibits, at least superficially, the contemporary crisis of meaning that has contributed to the development of symbolic anthropology.

It is precisely at this juncture that the Don Juan books, viewed in a Sapirian perspective, enter the arena of anthropological discourse. Castaneda's apprenticeship is based on a personal acknowledgment of meaninglessness. It develops against the backdrop of an increasingly unsatisfying "cultural system," that of the modern anthropologist as scientist. It is energized by Carlos' commitment to pursue personal affirmation through an experiential discipline that shapes as much as receives the imprint of its associated symbolics. Thus the work of Castaneda artfully acknowledges the existential challenge that lies at the base of Sapir's discussion of the genuine culture (1924). The tetralogy offers us the image of the warrior, as a shamanic reading of character with which to meet that challenge. Sapir wrote, apropos of human experiential creation of self and cultural reality, of the relationship between individual discipline and common tradition:

> Creation is a blending of form to one's will, not a manufacture of form ex nihilo . . . Sooner or later we shall have to get down to the humble task of exploring the depths of our own consciousness and dragging to the light what sincere bits of reflected experience we can find. These bits will not always be beautiful, they will not always be pleasing, but they will be genuine. (1924:418, 429)

The Don Juan tetralogy has given us a study of shamanism that is an iconography of iconoclasm and thus a work particularly appropriate for a postmodern humanity. That Castaneda has been able effectively to render a highly sophisticated and deeply meaningful primitive teaching to a contemporary audience through a personal encounter is a triumph of art, reflection, and will—and ultimately of humanistic anthropology. It is a fundamental validation of our disciplinary commitment to take the primitive seriously, on its own ground. On multiple levels, Castaneda has allowed the primitive shaman to enter into dialogue with the civilized anthropologist. As Geertz has said of symbolic anthropology, "Looked at in this way, the aim of anthropology is the enlargement of the universe of human discourse" (1973a:14).

Sapir's essays evince his fundamental concern with complex human beings, with their needs, purposes, and varying relationships to symbolics. The focus is on the individual human being as the empirical reality in relation to which our statements on culture must make sense. In the last analysis, the actual life of a human being is precisely what we seek to describe. In an important sense, an anthropological essay is nothing more nor less than a description of its readers in their concrete actualities. Its reception is dependent on its sensibility and on the sensitivities of the individuals who constitute its audience. If we wish to be taken seriously, we cannot simply offer up stories of collective self-congratulations or lost paradises. We cannot offer only images of human life as an illusory charade of order. Whereas Geertz, with justification, is reluctant seriously to consider the experiential basis upon which religious "beliefs" rest, this basis is precisely the heart of Castaneda's contribution to symbolic anthropology (Wilk 1977:86).

Even when confronting the seemingly impersonal domain of language, Sapir was able to see the experiences of individual human beings that were the sources of its creation. Witness the following statement from the final paragraph of his book, *Language*:

> Language is itself the collective art of expression, a summary of thousands upon thousands of individual intuitions. The individual goes lost in the collective creation, but his personal expression has left some trace in a certain give and flexibility that are inherent in all collective works of the human spirit. The language is ready, or can be quickly made ready, to define the artist's individuality. (1949:231)

Thus, contrary to Kroeber (1952a:148, 1952:108, 148), I would maintain that Sapir's final published statements on anthropology represent the culmination and maturation of his scholarly career:

> There is no reason why the culturalist should be afraid of the concept of personality, which must not, however, be thought of, as one inevitably does at the beginning of his thinking, as a mysterious entity resisting the historically given culture, but rather as a distinctive configuration of experience which tends to form a psychologically significant unit and which, as it accretes more and more symbols to itself, creates finally that cultural microcosm of which official "culture" is little more than a metaphorically and mechanically expanded copy . . . In short, the application of the personality point of view tends to minimize the bizarre or exotic in alien cultures and to reveal to us more and more clearly the broad human base on which all culture has been developed. The profound commonplace that all culture starts from the needs of a common humanity is believed in by anthropologists, but it is not demonstrated by their writings. . . . Culture is then not something given but something to be gradually and gropingly discovered. (1963b:595–96)

Through the years Sapir's professional posture increasingly exhibited the truth of a fundamental dynamic of crosscultural analysis: that by acknowledging and respecting the different in all its subtlety, we position ourselves to apprehend and appreciate the deeper unities. As Lao Tzu said, "If you would take from a thing, you must first give to it" (1963:95). Ruth L. Bunzel described the mature Sapir in the following manner: "No two individuals have precisely the same life experience, how can they share the same culture? He was fond of saying, 'There are as many cultures as there are individuals.' He proclaimed the study of the individual as the proper study of anthropologists" (1968:439). Sapir's perspective is not "almost anticultural," it is a solid framework upon which to build a contemporary appreciation of the human condition as the generic cultural condition. The Don Juan tetralogy reveals the potency of this conceptualization by illustrating the importance of "experiential irresolvability" (Sapir 1917:445) for symbolic anthropology.

The human-centered Sapirian cultural focus can help to resolve some of the difficulties encountered in the anthropological treatment of contemporary social life. Many scholars have commented on the heterogeneity of modern societies (see, for example, Pelto 1975, Wallace 1970). As Durkheim observed, "Thus, we make our way, little by little, toward a state, nearly achieved as of now, where the members of a single social group will have nothing in common among themselves except their humanity, except the constitutive attributes of the human person (personne humaine) in general" (1973:51). I believe that a hallmark of modernity as a culture type is the disappearance of many of the customary unities that contributed to the conceptualization of culture as distinctive "shared traits" of specific human groupings. This disappearance has led some anthropologists to advocate an abandonment of the "language " metaphor of culture. I believe that such an abandonment leads to the loss of a vital focus on meaningful human existence that constitutes the heart of symbolic anthropology (see, for example, Aberle 1960:14). It was the genius of Edward Sapir to realize that the postmodern challenge for cultural anthropology was the interpretive quest for the deeper unities of the cultural condition that set *human* being apart as a species-specific state. As human character and genuine culture are rooted in integrity, so Sapir realized that the analysis of the human condition through culture-talk could not abandon the ongoing quest for cultural universals that lie beneath and support the modern organization of diversity, the quest for an increased appreciation of our common humanity, without abandoning the obligation we have to posterity. He realized that as culture-talk begins and ends with the individual human being, it is the deeper inspection of human individuals that holds the secret to a postmodern conceptualization of culture in terms of a symbolics of meaning. To forsake such an interpretive enterprise is to forsake our commitment to the primitive. Stanley Diamond, articulated beautifully, in the following postmodern clarification, what constitutes knowledge of the primitive: "A sense of the minimally human, a sense of what is essential to being human" (1974:119).

If we look at contemporary theorists of culture within anthropology who have moved away from a language metaphor so as to deal with modern diversity, we see a clear failure of critical reflection. Aberle, the Peltos, and Wallace, for example, offer approaches to culture that, while helpful in organizing diversity, do so at the price of neglecting human emotional and cognitive wellbeing. Biological adaptation, contractual relationships, factory systems, and games are put forward as guiding metaphors for the appropriate anthropological conceptualization of the contemporary cultural context. I maintain that considerations of human character and consequence are buried beneath this welter of efficient strategies and organizational techniques. Questions of utlimate destination tend to be lost in a utilitarian maze designed to separate winners from losers. While such conceptualizations of diversity have value for anthropological analysis, if we seek actively to counter the dangers of ethnocentrism and absolutism, they must be complemented by a variety of human-centered perspectives that seek a subtle balance of diversity and uniformity along the lines of Sapir's language mataphor. As Sapir recognized, the question of how human existence is made possible must be balanced by the question of how it is made worthwhile — that is, genuine (1924). While our repertoire of paradigms must be capable of modeling the realities they seek to clarify, they must not all simply reflect our enculturative experience. It is vital for the future development of anthropology that its conceptual repertoire and research paradigms be varied enough to maintain the power not simply to reflect, but also to reflect upon, modern civilization, from a humane and critical crosscultural vantage point, the vantage point of culture-consciousness.

If Durkheim's (1933) "mechanical solidarity" and Redfield's (1953) "moral order" exhibit a highly limited applicability to analysis of contemporary state-organized societies, we cannot ignore this and proceed as if modern America, for example, were a primitive society. It would be equally foolish totally to abandon the traditional roots of our cultural conceptualizations for metaphoric seeds planted in our minds by life in modern political states of the Western world. Ironically, while the customary homogeneity envisioned by earlier anthropologists appears ever more barren as a source of contemporary cultural coneptualization, the postmodern world we seek to address on behalf of future generations demands imaginative exploration, interpretive studies of deep cultural commonalities that cut across regional and national borders. The postmodern world does not challenge anthropology simply to conceptualize national diversity. The international nature of contemporary human existence, an existence that takes place in increasingly interconnected political units possessing hitherto unimagined technological means of destruction, demands a critical postmodern address to a renewed sense of our common humanity.

Before the close of World War I, Sapir realized that the genuine anthropological challenge was to confront the deep complexities of the real human being, so as to reconstitute on a higher, more inclusive level, the sense of a shared humanity appropriate to a postmodern world. Throughout his theoretical corpus runs the implicit definition of culture as symbolically mediated experience, a definition that focuses at once on the concrete individual and the species as a whole, in terms of a deeply suggestive common humanity. Sapir realized that we must abandon the reifications, oversimplified reductions, and superficial orderings of politically enculturated anthropologists, of the anthropologist as expert, for the authoritatively complex human actualities that it is our professional mission symbolically to order— not just for others, but for ourselves as well. For the conceptualization of culture as symbolically mediated experience is equally and simultaneously applicable to both the anthropologist and the other human subjects of her or his inquiry. The implications of such a Sapirian approach have been depicted for us artfully through Castaneda's shamanic apprenticeship in the tetralogy. As Sapir realized, the anthropologist as humanist would have to give up some of the abstract elegance of the "expert," but would balance this loss with a great gain in personal engagement, genuine engagement with her or his profession and audience. Rather than viewing human beings as variations on a theme of culture, Sapir realized that we must give serious attention to perspectives that view cultures as variations on a theme of humanity. Sapir and Castaneda have indicated, each in his own fashion, that by focusing on the concrete human being, we can consider the problematics of meaningful human existence in a context of modern heterogeneity. The image of human existence as a personal, rather than simply collective, making of meaning has great value for contemporary anthropological study. I believe that the human-centered conceptualization of culture, as a historically and biographically given medium for the personal creation of a satisfying existence, rather than as a predetermined pattern for human development, is a vital and mature addition to our conceptual repertoire.

Edward Sapir realized that such a cultural focus on the individual human being of our experience inevitably would lead to a sincere consideration of the social as a meaningful and necessary extension and completion of the experienced self.* Through a courageous exploration of the reality of our life-worlds, our cultural realities, the pursuit of our common humanity, our personal experience of the universals of the relative cultural condition, inevitably would bring about, as well, a therapeutic anthropology. From this vantage point we can appreciate Don Juan's challenge to find a path with a heart, his emphasis on the need for affirmation rather than resignation. I am convinced that the portrait of shamanism as a making of meaning, human life as artistic performance, as poetry, is a real contribution to the future of anthropology. I am equally convinced that alienation and anomie are descriptions of personal cultural conditions and not acultural conceptualizations. Beyond the personally therapeutic, I believe that the Sapirian approach to culture, Sapir's understanding of the interpretive challenge faced by anthropology, will restore our Durkheimian appreciation of anthropology as moral science (see Rieff:1972). Edward Sapir's conceptualization of culture stands at the therapeutic crossroads of symbolic anthropology and psychological anthropology, and of the anthropology of religion and political anthropology. Furthermore, that crossroads is no less than a responsible, a consciously interpretive, moral science of culture.

I have stated previously that "Don Juan emerges as a spiritual master whose image of man offers a challenge and guide that a discipline devoted to the non-ethnocentric study of cultural phenomena cannot afford to dismiss lightly" (1972:922). In this spirit, I wish to conclude my discussion of a Sapirian perspective on culture and the

*See Don Genaro's remarks on his relationship to Don Juan (Castaneda 1971:312).

Don Juan quartet by grounding it in a brief consideration of human identity. I shall resist the temptation to consider human identity by focusing on Don Juan and the teachings. Rather I shall discuss a being about whom others may be less skeptical and a fictive identity with which I am quite familiar: myself as a Jew.

I was born to Jewish parents and will be treated as a Jew in my social world, regardless of my beliefs and practices, unless I consciously or unconsciously hide that fact of my birth. In this sense my identity has been historically, biographically, socially determined. However, it has not been culturally determined in a Sapirian sense. Such a human identity had only limited meaning to me, largely in terms of its historical and social distortions. My coming of age as a Jew was a very private affair. It involved a number of deeply moving private experiences that culminated in a meaningful, though by no means exclusive, affirmation and claim of my Jewish identity. Other individuals helped in this process as exemplary models of transformation, as makers of meaning, as powerful shamanic exemplifications of humanity, not primarily as participants in collective ritual.* My Bar Mitzvah, although a collective ritual marking a formal transition to adult status as a male Jew, had no such meaning for me. I remember it more in terms of Ruth Benedict's Kwakiutl potlatch (1959). Now, as a mature human being, having been born to Jewish parents, I can personally claim and affirm my Jewish identity for myself. To tell me that I am not Jewish because I do not keep a kosher home would be as absurd to me as putting Ishi in a museum. To say that I cannot be more than a Jew without denying my tribal history is equally absurd to me. I claim the right to interpret my own biography, my own reality, without denying my claim to my Jewish heritage. To deny me that right would be highly unfortunate, to say the least. Denials of this sort flow from a failure to see that human identity is not simply "given," "culturally determined," the result of a determinant social process that is to be certified by the professional anthropologist. Human identity is, in important respects—Sapirian

---

*Hsu's (1971:27) distinction between role and affective referents for human needs is closely related to the idea of personal meaning I am emphasizing.

respects, shamanic respects — a matter of self-assertion, the result of personal efforts and experiences. As Sapir stressed, the human being is not simply a reflection of culture but also its creator, interpreter, experiencer, and evaluator. The anthropological tradition of culture as shared traits, represented by Beals' position, is too shallow to claim exclusive privilege in the contemporary cultural context. Ultimately it forces us as anthropologists to deny to the human being the right of meaningful reinterpretation, when this is precisely the task of postmodern humanity, and therefore of humanistic anthropology, and one of the few valid sources of contemporary heterogeneity. For anthropology to conduct a charade of authority in the contemporary world is seriously to impair the vitality and validity of cultural traditions as historically bequeathed mediums for human existence, by positioning ourselves in opposition to the very forces our own anthropological discipline should have taught us to appreciate. As Lucy S. Dawidowicz proclaimed in the concluding paragraph of an essay on Jewish identity: "Goethe once said that only he earns his freedom and existence who daily conquers them. The reward of being Jewish lies in defining oneself, not in being defined. The gift is in possessing one's heritage and in affirming one's existence on one's own ground" (1977:31).

Don Juan's image of the warrior is a shamanic reading of primitive character appropriate to a postmodern discussion of integrity and culture. Through his imaginative account of a shamanic apprenticeship, Carlos Castaneda has given to anthropology a meaningful interpretation of a primitive character that is an instructive possibility for postmodern humanity. He has accomplished this by taking the primitive seriously on its own terms. By looking at the tetralogy in the Sapirian light, we can come to appreciate the rich interpretive challenge that awaits a postmodern anthropology dedicated to a teaching profession. That wise old master Evans-Pritchard knew that the way to refresh our vision of primitive cultures was to focus on the fundamental matter of translation (1965:7–8, 12–14). Edward Sapir had this same insight and knew that when we take culture to the level of the human being as symbolically mediated experience, the challenge for a postmodern humanity is one of personal translation or sense making, the shamanic challenge. In such a context he realized that a teaching anthropology, a humanistic anthropology, a postmodern anthropology, must seek out the challenge to meaningfully reintroduce postmodern humanity to itself through the establishment of a consciously acknowledged and highly and personally responsible interpretive tradition, the anthropologist as mythmaker (see Richardson 1975).

My vision of anthropology first appeared, and is often renewed, in the classroom rather than in the Sonoran desert. It is a dream of knowing and sharing something of human worth, by taking seriously, anthropologically, the widest range of human creations. Surely, if Don Juan has taught us anything, it is that true human freedom comes with heightened awareness and the assumption of personal responsibility. As Edward Sapir realized, we will find the true meaning of such a word as "love" not simply in a dictionary, but more fully in the lived experience of our existence. I cherish this anthropological insight as I cherish the growing realization that as I define the shaman, so I define myself.

7 A Note on American Democracy and American Anthropology

In an address entitled "Democracy and Intellectual Freedom," Franz Boas, a founder of both American anthropology and its doctrine of cultural relativism, observed the following:

A bigoted majority may be as dangerous to free thought as the heavy hand of a dictator. For this reason we must demand fullest freedom of expression, so that our youth may be prepared for an intelligent use of the privileges and duties of citizenship. Notwithstanding all the lapses of which we may have been guilty, the ideal of our democracy is freedom of thought and expression. This is clearly expressed in the Declaration of Independence and in the Bill of Rights; free speech, free assembly, free press prove that our aim is to strive for intellectual freedom. Science certainly cannot live in an atmosphere of restraint. In democratic societies it has largely succeeded in shaking off the chains of dogma, at least in so far as the natural sciences are concerned. We still have much to learn in regard to freedom of research and expression in the social sciences, but at least we have the will to achieve it. The disposition to consider as heresy a view different from that in vogue and to incite passionate persecution of those holding it must be overcome. If we wish to fight prejudice, the results of honest research, whatever they may be, must be accessible to all. (Boas 1969a:175–6)

As Boas implies, freedom of religion is itself dependent on a broader intellectual freedom that imbues the First Amendment guarantees of our Constitution with the Enlightenment commitment to naturalistic knowledge and reason and to public, secular education. Historically, our basic freedoms, including our freedom of religion, are the result of the application of naturalistic thought to human history. As Justice Joseph Story wrote, in regard to the government exclusion from religious affairs, in his commentaries on the Constitution:

It was under a solemn consciousness of the dangers from ecclesiastical ambition, the bigotry of spiritual pride, and the intolerance of sects . . . exemplified in our domestic as well as foreign annals, that it was deemed advisable to exclude from the national government all power to act upon the subject. (Witt 1980:79)

It is time we came to realize that religion must, for its own good and the good of our society, exclude itself from acting on our secular form of government. On the occasion of the Virginia legislature's passage in December 1785 of the "Act for religious Freedom," written by Thomas Jefferson, James Madison wrote that the act "extinguishes forever the ambitious hope of making laws for the human mind" (Beth 1958:68).

As a scientific humanist, I believe that we have an obligation that comes with the religious freedom we enjoy in our republic. This obligation is for the citizen as political participant, to exercise self-restraint, particularly the disciplining of emotions, in the service of the naturalistic intellect. This restraint is the basis of our contemporary faith in democracy, a faith in natural reason to guide the political pursuit of the common good. I wish briefly to explore this obligation in relation to American anthropology. The exercise of individual self-restraint that American anthropologists must make as citizens of the United States is equally necessary for their pursuit of the naturalistic investigation of human affairs that is the discipline of anthropology. To the extent that anthropologists can control their emotional lives in the service of naturalistic reason, empirical investigation, and empathic understanding of the other, they authenticate the legitimacy of their claims to being a science of humanity. Not surprisingly, the major anthropological teaching bearing on the moral, political, and religious affairs of humankind in general, the doctrine of cultural relativism, as implied in the works of Franz Boas and popularly associated with the writings of his student Melville Herskovits, emphasizes the traditional, biographical, and emotional, i.e., the nonrational, basis, in the naturalistic intellectual sense, of most human values and beliefs. As enunciated by Herskovits, the principle of cultural relativism is: "Judgments are based on experience, and experience is interpreted by each individual in terms of his own enculturation." From this principle, Herskovits puts forward for consideration as a rational idea, the value of tolerance of human diversity. Such tolerance depends upon the same reasoned exercise of self-control over deeply held emotional convictions that the individual citizen must cultivate to protect our freedoms in general. As the scientist becomes the scientific humanist, daring to connect "is" and "ought," a natural moral discourse worthy of our political arena emerges. It is my contention that American anthropologists as United States citizens have an obligation to educate our citizenry to the substance of cultural relativism. In this way we can aid the members of our republic to exercise proper self-restraint as they move from the sphere of their religious life to the sphere of their political life, from their properly private to the properly public existence. To do so is to insure our own disciplinary future as well, for both American anthropology and the United States political doctrine of separation of church and state are precious cultural manifestations of our Enlightenment commitment to naturalistic reason and knowledge. To understand our nation's history is to understand vital aspects of the fortunate history of American anthropology. It is time that anthropology and anthropologists begin to repay with greater generosity their historical and personal debts.

In 1939 Boas wrote a statement on "The Role of the Scientist," in which he said:

> Can we say conscientiously that scientists are not influenced by demagogues, catch-words and slogans? Is it not rather true that a great many of us, who may be clear thinkers in our own fields, are so little versed in public affairs, so much confined in our narrow field, that we are swayed by passionate appeals to outworn ideals or to a selfish interest that runs counter to the interest of the people? So when we speak of the need for education do not let us forget that we have to educate ourselves. Uncontrolled emotionalism is the greatest enemy of intellectual freedom. To educate people to rational ideals without destroying their emotional life is one of the great and difficult tasks of our times. (Boas 1969b:217)

American anthropology can strengthen both itself and its supporting society by embodying the voice of natural reason and knowledge in human affairs through an increasing engagement in the public issues of our democratic republic. This mission is in keeping with the efforts of Franz Boas, Ruth Benedict, Melville Herskovits, and many

others. As the historian Peter Gay notes in regard to the Enlightenment philosophers:

> The philosophers' refusal to construct a theory of progress . . . turns out
> to be a refusal to be complacent about the effects that the accumulation
> of knowledge might have on the shape of life. The harmony between
> knowledge and improvement was not automatic, or inevitable, it was a
> demand that runs through the philosophers' conception of what social
> science must be. In their eyes, scientific detachment and reformist involve-
> ment belonged together, the application of reason to society meant that
> knowledge and welfare, knowledge and freedom, knowledge and hap-
> piness must be made into inseparable allies. (1978:322)

It is my belief that American anthropology and our democratic republic, with its limited secular state and larger spiritual community,
also must be made into the inseparable allies that they, in fact, historically have been. As a United States citizen and as a cultural anthropologist, I object to many of the activities of Jerry Falwell, his
former Moral Majority, and the rejuvenated Religious Right in general. My objections as citizen and as anthropologist flow from the
same source, the eighteenth-century Enlightenment commitment to
naturalistic reason and empirical fact.

My thesis is that the basis for legitimate anthropological knowledge, the evidences and reasoning processes that legitimate my belief
in anthropological knowledge, are the same evidences and reasoning
processes that legitimate the actions of our goverment as established
by our country's founders. By establishing a political doctrine of
separation of church and state, these creators provided for a society
whose political life would be viewed as limited in nature and secular
in thought and action. Following from this original intention, I con-
tend, all informed and mature members of United States society, in
their political capacity as citizens, should strive to be naturalistic in
the modern sense of logical reasoning in relation to empirical evidence. The American anthropologist can contribute to the American
democratic republic by helping to educate the citizenry about the need
for, and methods and results of, naturalistic reason applied to human
affairs.

I wish to clarify what I mean by modern naturalistic reasoning,
by briefly considering a contemporary case in point. The value of

a "right to life" is currently being put forward in the political arena of our nation as the basis for the prohibition of abortion as legal conduct. As this value is not agreed upon by all citizens of the United States, nor established in any specific way in our Constitution, which sets forth in a minimal fashion the consensually held values upon which American society, as represented by the United States government, was founded and legitimated, discussion of a "right to life" must confine itself to considering this value as a naturalistically rational idea. To do less is to violate the doctrine of separation of church and state and to threaten the delicate social fabric of our nation, upon whose proper function our freedoms as American citizens are based. Specifically, the curtailment of individual liberty attendant upon the abolition of abortion, the individual liberty guaranteed by the values clearly enunciated in our Constitution, can be justified politically only on the basis of naturalistic thought and evidence.

In a television message broadcast in Williamsport, Pennsylvania, on Sunday, 7 March 1982, Jerry Falwell spoke in favor of making abortions illegal. Using a misreading of the biblical text in which Nehemiah advises "to seek the welfare of the children" (a misreading since Nehemiah was not, as Falwell implied, speaking of the children of all humanity but rather of the children of Israel), Falwell went on to offer the following four reasons for the advocated political action:

1. Children are important to God.
2. Massive abortion creates a low view of human life.
3. The Judgment of God is going to fall on those people who commit abortion.
4. We are going to meet the aborted fetuses (or, as he called them, "children") one day in heaven, and they will charge us with murdering them.

Only his second reason, "massive abortion creates a low view of human life," is a naturalistic assertion rooted in modern rationality and, theoretically at least, subject to empirical investigation. As such it is the only reason of the four that validly can be raised in our political debates regarding abortion if we are to be true to our doctrine of the separation of church and state. It is worth noting that even this reason, if empirically established, could not in and of itself establish a rational secular basis for denying freedom of choice but could at least contribute a legitimate component to rational consideration of the proposed legislation.

To say that the other three reasons do not constitute a valid basis for political discourse in the United States is not to say that its citizens do not have the right to believe in these reasons. This right, of course, also is protected by the doctrine of separation of church and state contained in the First Amendment to our Constitution, which guarantees to members of our society freedom of religion. But it is to say that the same First Amendment, as established and interpreted throughout our history by the Supreme Court, also provides for the separation of church and state—i.e., a limited secular state whose legitimate operations are to be guided by naturalistic reason and evidence within the forms provided by the Constitution. Thus, while to prohibit such beliefs clearly violates the First Amendment's guarantee of religious freedom, to make non-naturalistic reasoning the basis of political action does, too. And that same amendment prohibits our limited secular government from establishing a religion. Tolerance begins with the realization that genuine freedom is based on choice. Our Constitution gives our government no freedom in regard to the secular nature of its legitimacy, functioning, and purpose. If government is not to establish a religion, it must deny itself the luxury of indulging in religious reasoning. In the United States, the freedom of religion, like all rights, implies and can be sensibly understood only in relation to its attendant responsibilities.

Contrary to the beliefs of Jerry Falwell and the Religious Right, the freedom of religion in our democracy does not imply the responsibility to convert the whole society or its representative secular state to a particular sectarian interpretation of a particular religious tradition. On the contrary, it implies the responsibility of each citizen who enjoys the freedom of religion to respect that same freedom in the lives of her or his fellow citizens. Specifically, and most germane to the present discussion, it implies the admittedly difficult political obligation as citizens to rethink our religious life as it relates to our political life, our public life as it relates to our private life, our emotionally held values and beliefs as they relate to our secularly rational naturalistic considerations of public issues.

It is our freedoms that give meaning to our private lives. How

Democracy and Anthropology 99

ironic if our public life diminishes our freedom through an unjustified concern with our private lives. Such imposition on our personhood is literally "self" destructive. Those who genuinely understand the historical and rational basis of freedom of religion, and its intimate connection with the doctrine of separation of church and state, will practice the difficult, indeed heroic, discipline of rational self-restraint on emotion, in their capacity as participants in our nation's political life. It is this exercise of self-restraint in regard to one's feelings which Emile Durkheim rationally understood as being in opposition to egotism and which in fact underlies all human social life. This same self-restraint as regards affect is the fundamental support of the freedom of religion we enjoy as citizens of a democratic republic. It is, as well, a necessary prerequisite to the naturalistic rationality that moved our nation's founders, in keeping with the Enlightenment tradition, to establish a limited secular state through our Constitution. This limited secular state is not to be confused with United States society as a whole; indeed, the identification of the state with society is typical of totalitarian nations, which the framers of our Constitution, in their wisdom, sought to avoid.

The Religious Right does not understand this need for separation. To do so is to understand why our First Amendment not only guarantees freedom of religion and provides for a secular state, but also grants to us the freedoms of speech, press, assembly, and the right to petition our government for a redress of grievances. All of these "natural rights" granted by our form of government are the fruits of the humane disciplining of emotional life so as to allow naturalistic reason and experience to prevail in the political life of our nation, to allow human intellect to be guided by natural reason and natural experience in its efforts to conceive and create a sensible and humane social order through the establishment of a finite and limited form of government. Our secular state is a rational attempt to insure the liberties we so cherish, including the freedom of religion that Jerry Falwell and the Religious Right so abuse.

Jerry Falwell likes to call to mind the image of "godless Communism," but he does not understand that naturalistic thought can be as emotionally distorted as religious thought can be. How can he understand this, when he does not recognize the emotional basis of much of his own reasoning? Communism can and does have its crude emotional true believers, who, like many religious persecutors, pave the way to hell for other people with their own good intentions. Falwell does not understand that the rational protection against the religious persecution that is found in a totalitarian nation such as the Soviet Union is a limited secular state that does not see its interests as coterminous with, or, worse, as superior to, those of its individual private citizens. Indeed, in such a totalitarian system it does not make sense to speak of a private citizen or of a society that is more inclusive in its functioning than the state. The proper functioning of government is not to save the souls of the members of society, but to coordinate and facilitate the liberties they enjoy in their private lives, their personal pursuits. The proper government therefore constitutes the political sphere through the establishment of a naturalistically rational system of laws, regulations, and bureaucracies that facilitate orderly social life in the service of consensually acknowledged public values, so as to promote the just pursuit of private lives by its citizens. The best defense against state persecution of religion is not, as Falwell and the Religious Right believe, a government that supports a particular version of a historical religious tradition, but rather one that acknowledges personal life as basic and its support as primary. Even a state that supports all religious traditions would not be a good defense of freedom of belief. For such a state would be a religion unto itself, in its power to determine what belief systems are or are not genuine religious belief systems, not to mention the possible infringements on the human rights of nonbelievers. Witness the confused and confusing discussions of "cults" and "brain washing" that tend to define religions on the quantitative basis of the number of adherents.

Far better, far more rational, to create a state that envisions itself as limited in function, by limiting it to using naturalistic reason and knowledge, embodied in law and due process, as the basis upon which it can justify actions. Such a state is the true home of the personal sensemaker, the one who wishes to pursue genuine cultural existence. As most of us know, though we may not admit it to ourselves, happiness is a complex and personal discovery. As a scientific humanist, I believe that the freedom claimed by Socrates, the freedom to act through one's own thinking and think through one's own acting, is essential for the authentic pursuit of happiness.

Thus, a naturally legitimate state must not dictate, but rather must facilitate, the pursuit of happiness. This is an entitlement that each citizen of the United States has a right to expect, given our Constitution. Such a state must be neutral in regard to matters of religion, so as to protect all our freedoms of thought and action, including our freedom in relation to religion. In 1970, Chief Justice Warren Burger stated the following in regard to government neutrality in terms of the First Amendment separation of church and state:

> The course of constitutional neutrality in this area cannot be an absolutely straight line; rigidity could well defeat the basic purpose of these provisions, which is to insure that no religion be sponsored or favored, none commanded and none prohibited. The general principle deducible from the First Amendment and all that has been said by the Court is this: that we will not tolerate either governmentally established religion or governmental interference with religion. Short of those expressly proscribed governmental acts there is room for play in the joints productive of a benevolent neutrality which will permit religious exercise to exist without sponsorship and without interference.
>
> Each value judgement under the Religion Clauses must therefore turn on whether particular acts in question are intended to establish or interfere with religious beliefs and practices or have the effect of doing so. Adherence to the policy of neutrality that derives from an accommodation of the Establishment and Free Exercise Clauses has prevented the kind of involvement that would tip the balance toward government control of churches or governmental restraint on religious practice. (Witt 1980:79)

While I do not disagree with Justice Burger, as far as he goes regarding government neutrality, I am arguing that the separation of church and state allows, and indeed requires, the government to be secular and naturalistically rational in reasoning and evidence, while being neutral; this is the intention of our Constitution. The secular state is not to be understood in terms of the absence of religious belief, but rather in terms of the presence of naturalistic reason and knowledge. Secular character in no way necessarily implies the secular society of Communist totalitarianism, any more than the fanaticism of the Inquisition implied that heaven on earth was coming. Government neutrality in regard to religions is, in an important sense, to be understood as a consequence of its self-imposed limitation to naturalistic thought and evidence. To put it in terms of a principle: in those aspects of human affairs where naturalistic reason and knowledge are not applicable, there government should not stray. In the all-too-real world of the emotional needs and cognitive concerns that constitute important dimensions of our private lives and views, the wisdom of our democratic republican form of government is to grant personal liberty rather than coercively to impose ultimately arbitrary collective solutions. Government's social concern is regulating legality, not morality, and so government has tremendous problems securing its own moral operation. The legal and moral domains are set apart in our form of government by their susceptibility to modern rational reflection and research. Morality only enters the sphere of legality in our country through the consensually recognized human freedoms that are embodied as political values in our Constitution and so form the basis of our state's legitimacy and the moral basis for our being law-abiding in general. To say this is merely to point out the obvious correctness of Wittgenstein's distinction between natural thought and supernatural beliefs and practices. For example, it was only when biological research established the harmful effects of cigarette smoking on the human organism that our government had a legitimate right to involve itself in the depopularization of cigarette smoking. Until that point, it was, under our Constitution, legitimately none of its business.

This conception of the state in terms of natural reason and knowledge is not my own invention. It can be seen clearly in the writings of such founding leaders as Thomas Jefferson. In *Notes on Virginia*, he says the following in relation to the state:

> The rights of conscience we never submitted, we could not submit. We are answerable for them to our God . . . Reason and free inquiry are the only effectual agents against error. Give a loose to them, they will support the true religion by bringing every false one to their tribunal, to the test of their investigation. They are the natural enemies of error, and of error only.
>
> . . . Subject opinions to coercion: Whom will you make your inquisitors? Fallible men; men governed by bad passions, by private as well as public reasons. And why subject it to coercion? To produce uniformity . . . Is uniformity attainable? Millions of innocent men, women, and children, since the introduction of Christianity have been burnt, tortured,

fined, imprisoned; yet we have not advanced one inch toward uniformity. What has been the effect of coercion? To make one half the world fools, and the other half hypocrites. To support roguery and error all over the earth. (Cited in Pfeiffer 1953:94–95)

In *Notes on Religion,* Jefferson states:

> The care of every man's soul belongs to himself. But what if he neglects the care of it? Well what if he neglects the care of his health or estate, which more clearly relates to the state. Will the magistrate make a law that he shall not be poor or sick? Laws provide against injury from others; but not from ourselves. God himself will not save men against their wills . . . If a magistrate command me to bring my commodity to a publick store house I bring it because he can indemnify me if he erred and I thereby lose it; but what indemnification can be given one for the kingdom of heaven? I cannot give up my guidance to the magistrate, because he knows no more of the way to heaven that I do and is less concerned to direct me right that I am to go right. (Pfeiffer 1953:94–95)

Our nation is the child of a secular political rebellion whose goal was the improvement of human government over men and women. Our democratic republican form of government is not the cultural consequence of a religious revival, but of the Enlightenment commitment to the life of the modern human mind, the commitment to natural knowledge and natural reasoning. We should not allow a contemporary failure of nerve to blind us to the historical fact that the separation of church and state is a brilliant manifestation of this commitment to naturalistic human reason for the administration of the public affairs of a modern society. After all, scientific research can more assuredly ascertain the objective basis for racial beliefs and the consequences of racial discrimination on the human psyche, than can Bob Jones III through his scriptural interpretations. Naturalistic reason and research can ascertain more assuredly the natural consequences of malnutrition on the health and development of a human infant than Jerry Falwell, Jessie Helms, or Ronald Reagan can objectively ascertain the godliness of government.

The contemporary mind in the postmodern world demands and deserves logical argument, based on naturalistic concepts supported by empirical investigation, not self-assured textual interpretations. Our country's early leaders built this demand into our Constitution through the separation of church and state. With such natural knowledge in hand and disseminated to my fellow citizens, I choose, as did our founders and their supporters in revolutionary society, to place my faith in the common humanity of my fellow citizens, in their personal sense of spirituality and of right and wrong, to guide their private lives. As Jefferson stressed, our behaviour is first and foremost our own business, not that of a fanatic, a charlatan, or a mere politician.

James Madison wrote in *The Federalist*:

> But why is the experiment of an extended republic to be rejected merely because it may comprise what is new? Is it not the glory of the people of America, that whilst they have paid a decent regard to the opinions of former times and other nations, they have not suffered a blind veneration of antiquity, for custom, or for names, to overrule the suggestions of their own good sense, the knowledge of their own situation, and the lessons of their own experience? To this manly spirit, posterity will be indebted for the possession, and the world for the example of the numerous innovations displayed on the American theater, in favor of private rights and public happiness. (Cited in Gay 1978:566–67)

The historian Peter Gay comments on this statement:

> Nothing could epitomize the spirit of the Enlightenment more beautifully than this oratorical flight, with its declared openness to experiment unfettered by its respect for the past, its disdain for authority, and its reliance on autonomous reason, good sense, and experience, all for the sake of freedom and happiness. (Gay 1978:567)

Jerry Falwell has said the following regarding one of the greatest "innovations displayed on the American theater," the doctrine of separation of church and state, in his book *Listen, America!*:

> The intention of our Founding Fathers was to protect American people from an established government church, a church that would be controlled by the government and paid for by the taxpayers. Our Founding Fathers sought to avoid this favoritism by separating church and state in function. This does not mean they intended a government devoid of God or the guidance found in Scripture. . . . To separate personal religious preference from a forced establishment of religion is far different from separating godliness from government. (Falwell 1980:53–54)

Contrary to the historical interpretation of Jerry Falwell, the separation of godliness from government is precisely what our democratic republic is about. However, I wish to stress, contrary to the assertions of Falwell, Sen. Jesse Helms, and former President Reagan, that this separation is not an attack on godliness. It is rather a recognition that godliness is a private matter to be pursued voluntarily by society members in their enjoyment of personal liberties, including the freedom of religion. The separation of church and state is our basic protection of religious freedom, and any encroachment on the separation is a major threat to the religious freedom we enjoy as United States citizens. However, the separation, contrary to Jerry Falwell's interpretation, also protects the limited and secular state in its legitimate exercise of natural reason and knowledge. The major responsibility of our government officials is not to be saintly in the reckoning of any particular interpretation of a particular historical religious tradition, but rather to be rationally competent in the modern naturalistic sense of reason and knowledge and to be respectful of our laws and Constitution, regardless of the origin of that respect. In our form of government, officials are not to use non-naturalistic categories of thought and non-naturalistic evidences. They are not to be guided by values other than those enshrined in our Constitution or established on a naturalistically rational basis and consensually adopted. Certainly we are not to be guided by emotionally satisfying and/or convincing values and beliefs that cannot be defended rationally in a naturalistic sense. As James Madison states in *The Federalist*:

> If men were angels, no government would be necessary. If angels were to govern men, neither external nor internal controls on government would be necessary. In forming a government which is to be administered by men over men, the great difficulty lies in this: You must first enable the government to control the governed; and in the next place oblige it to control itself. A dependence on the people is, no doubt, the primary control on the Government. (Hamilton et al. 1847:298–9)

This dependence on the people to control their government is not, as the Religious Right believes, a license to impose one's own views on the secular state, but rather an obligation to scrutinize one's beliefs and actions in the political sphere, from the modern perspective of naturalistic reason and knowledge. To the extent that our citizenry can be relied upon to distinguish their emotional lives from their intellectual lives, and to control their affective lives in the name of naturalistic reason and American democracy, our government will be able to exercise self-control and our individual liberties best be insured. We return to the truism that a democracy is only as strong as its educated electorate.

As a scientific humanist, I believe that the so called "right to life" and the attempt to define abortion as murder are contemporary manifestations of uncontrolled emotionalsim that do great harm to many of our most vulnerable citizens. To treat the human tragedy of abortion as murder is cruel and unusual punishment. To attack sex education and contraception, while bestowing the rights of a human being on a fetus, is religious fanaticism that ignores a logical consideration of the facts. To focus on the minimal suffering of a fetus, an unrealized human potential, while ignoring the massive sufferings of actual human beings all around us, is misguided at best. The abortion controversy is a good example of a situation in which the relationship between "is" and "ought" should guide our moral thinking.

Nobody wants to have an abortion, as nobody wants to be poor. The "Right-to-Life" movement would do better to concern itself with the quality of human experience rather than with inappropriately extending our definition of human being to an entity that clearly exhibits none of the capacities which logicoempirically define our human cultural condition. A seed is not a tree, nor is a pregnant unwed teenager, a mother. Our bodies are not the property of the state. We should not allow our government, or our culture, to be changed in these harsh and inhumane ways in the name of particular interpretations of particular supernatural traditions.

In his essay "Education," Franz Boas observed:

> Automatic actions based on the habits of early childhood are most stable. The firmer the habits that are instilled into the child the less they are subject to reasoning, the stronger is their emotional appeal. If we wish to educate children to unreasoned mass action, we must cultivate set habits of action and thought. If we wish to educate them to intellectual and emotional freedom care must be taken that no unreasoned action takes such

habitual hold upon them that a serious struggle is involved in the attempt to cast it off. (1932:184)

Boas believed that both the scientist and the intellectual were subject to the effects of habits of action and thought. Speaking of scientists, he noted, "We are apt to follow the habitual activites of our fellows without a careful examination of the fundamental ideas from which their actions spring. Conformity in action has for its sequel conformity in thought. The emancipation from current thought is for most of us as difficult in science as it is in everyday life" (1932:205–206). Boas was committed to freedom of thought as a primary goal of contemporary education. He saw the necessity of cultivating strength of character and intellect so as to avoid replacing conventionalism with chaos. He saw the need for critical evaluation of the past but understood that to evaluate was not necessarily to banish. He firmly believed that freedom of thought could thrive only in a society that truly valued freedom of action, of choice; for he saw free thought and action as two parts of one living process. Speaking of religion, he noted a deep paradox:

> Families and schools which assiduously cultivate the tenents of a religious faith and of a religious ceremonial and surround them with an emotional halo raise, on the whole, a generation that follows the same path . . . In the majority of individuals who grow up under these conditions a new, distinct viewpoint is not brought out with sufficient vigor to make it clear that theirs is not freely chosen, but imposed upon them; and if strange ideas are presented, the emotional appeal of the thoughts that are part of their nature is sufficient to make any rationalization of the habitual attitude acceptable, except to those of strong intellect and character. To say the least, the cultivation of formal religious attitudes in family and school makes difficult religious freedom (1932:186–87).

Ours is a society of varied ethnic and religious backgrounds. It is a society of varied beliefs, interests, and identifications. Such a heterogeneous society must seek its future wellbeing through humane logicoempirical thought and dialogue. The imposition of the emotionally held convictions of some, no matter how deeply held, upon the lives of all is a serious mistake. Religiously motivated political movements in the contemporary world are, and will continue to be, a threat to the hard-won, precious, and fragile freedoms of natural humanity.

CONCLUSION

8 Humor and Culture: Anthropology and Human Consciousness

There are critical moments in the development of many disciplines when professional disagreements occur that will have far-reaching implications for the future. Often the full implications of such a disagreement are not understood even by the participants, substantial portions of whose life's work and thought still lie ahead of them. One such occasion in American anthropology was a disagreement in print between Alfred Kroeber and Edward Sapir regarding the conceptualization of anthropology as a historical science. While Kroeber at the time had not yet fully clarified his own thinking on the distinction between the concepts of society and culture, his ideas on culture were to become the decisive ones, in several significant respects, for the future development of the discipline. The exchange I refer to took place in 1917 in the pages of the *American Anthropologist*. In that year, Kroeber published an essay, "The Superorganic," which evoked a reply from Sapir entitled "Do We Need a 'Superorganic'?"

Kroeber observed thirty-five years later, "What the essay really protests is the blind shuttling back and forth between an equivocal 'race' and an equivocal 'civilization'" (1952:2). In the essay, Kroeber was not so much attacking racial prejudice as he was trying to establish the human social, or, more precisely, cultural, reality as worthy of "autonomous recognition." By that characteristically ambivalent phrase, Kroeber meant something very different from the anthropological humanism later to be expressed by Margaret Mead and her teacher, Ruth Benedict, who had been heavily influenced by Sapir's thinking. When Ruth Benedict spoke of "culture-consciousness" (1959), she did so in the belief that anthropology could provide the contemporary mind with a self-understanding, a transformed self-consciousness, that was simultaneously a transformed sense of human society, for she viewed cultural being as a psychosocial reality. To her mind, human society was an expression of human freedom and creativity. Behind the taken-for-granted impersonal sense of society lay the conscious realization that, as cultural animals, humankind had shaped its specific social destinies and cultural natures in history. To realize this—to become fully aware of human beings as cultural animals, of the self as a cultural animal, as the product of enculturation—was to rediscover the creative power and natural moral responsibility inherent in the human condition, considered logicoempirically. Thus, culture-consciousness intimately tied our thinking on humanity to our thinking on society, tied the personal to the customary. *Patterns of Culture* begins with the statement, "Anthropology is the study of human beings as creatures of society" (1959:1), and goes on to consider different ways of life, cultures, as "personality writ large." As Margaret Mead was to observe twenty-four years after its publication, "I believe *Patterns of Culture* has lived because of [Benedict's] robust conviction that a knowledge of how culture works gives to human beings a greater control over their own future than they have ever known before" (1959b:x).

For his part, Alfred Kroeber was little interested in human society and sociality. As he remarked in 1952 in regard to his essay, "The Possibility of a Social Psychology," written in 1918: "I, in 1918, for all my talking about social psychology, was interested in culture and very little in social interrelations. In fact, next to culture, I was then and am now much more interested in the qualities and motivations of individuals than what human beings do to one another in groups" (1952:52). Precisely because Kroeber never appreciated that culture was the conceptual intermediary between individual and groups, between personality and society, he never was able to integrate his own interest in culture with his interest in the individual, nor to understand the career trajectory of Edward Sapir. While Kroeber wrote a good deal on culture, he left us with very little in regard to his thinking on the individual.

Kroeber's own career was already foreshadowed in "The Superorganic," in which he announced a wish to replace a biological determinism, a reading of human history in terms of heredity, with a consideration of human history that focused on the products of human mentality, human cultural capacity, to the exclusion of human mentality, human attitudes, emotions, sentiments, and motivations, themselves. Kroeber acknowledged that "heredity operates in the domain of mind as well as that of the body" (1917:40). However, he insisted that "mentality relates to the individual. The social or cultural on the other hand is in its essence non-individual. Civilization, as such, begins only where the individual ends" (ibid). While Leslie White (1959) saw the individual and thus psychology as relevant to anthropology only to the extent that it revealed the human ability to carry culture, specifically the ability to appreciate symbols, Kroeber viewed the individual and psychology in a complementary relation, primarily in terms of the human ability to produce in the sense of "set in motion," culture. As he clearly stated, "The reason why mental heredity has so little if anything to do with civilization, is that civilization is not mental action but a body or stream of products of mental exercise" (1917:42).

While Kroeber shared with Benedict an aesthetic appreciation of human cultural creativity, he never truly understood *Patterns of Culture*, returning to a consideration of it at various points in his career after initially reviewing it for the *American Anthropologist* (1935, 1952, 1963). In that initial review, he quoted Benedict's statement that "we do not need a plank of configuration written into the platform of an ethnological school" (1935:689), expressing puzzlement over why the discussions of cultural patterns were cast largely in terms of what he described as "psychiatric configurations" (1935:689). He went on to observe that "there is likely to be a residuum of misimpression that her general concept of patterns means nearly the same thing as her special type of configurations" (1935:690). But this is precisely the case. Kroeber's own impersonal conception of culture seems to have blinded him to the fact that Benedict, like Sapir before her, held no such impersonal view of cultural reality. Indeed, if we proceed just twenty-four pages further in *Patterns of Culture*, we find Benedict clearly stating that "the problem of the individual is not clarified by stressing the antagonism between culture and the individual, but by stressing their mutual reinforcement. This rapport is so close that it is not possible to discuss patterns of culture without considering specifically their relation to individual psychology" (1959:254–55).

If we look back at Sapir's 1917 reply to Kroeber's "The Superorganic," we find him making a closely related point:

It is true that the content of an individual's mind is so overwhelmingly molded by the social traditions to which he is heir that the purely individual contribution of even markedly original minds is apt to seem swamped in the whole culture. Furthermore, the dead level of compromise necessitated by the clashing of thousands of wills, few of them of compelling potency, tends to sink the social importance of any one of them into insignificance. All this is true in the main. And yet it is always the individual that really thinks and acts and dreams and revolts. (1917:441–42)

However, Kroeber could not understand Sapir any better than he was to understand Benedict. Even more than Benedict's, Sapir's developing thought, though impressively consistent from 1917 until his death in 1939, remained an enigma to Kroeber, who felt compelled to ponder it at various times throughout his own career. He went as far as to say the following in 1947:

A contradiction remains unresolved between the body of Sapir's actual culturo-linguistic work and the several programmatic papers of his latter years in which he seemed to assert that culture is fully meaningful only in terms of individual psychiatric personality. This view can possibly be explained as a personal reaction to a sense of ego frustration finally induced in him by years of preoccupation with cultural and linguistic forms. (1947:108)

Despite Kroeber"s discomfort with Leslie White's "culturology," revolving around the latter's focus on human behavior and needs, cultural materialism, his physical scientistic reductivism, and the search for casual explanations, there is a fundamental logical continuity between Kroeber's "The Superorganic" (1917) and White's "The Concept of Culture" (1959).* This continuity is clearly revealed in their shared extreme cultural determinism, manifest in their impersonal conceptualizations of culture. As Leslie White bluntly put it, in his typical scientific phraseology, "A people's behavior is a response to, a function of, their culture. The culture is the independent, the behavior the dependent, variable; as the culture varies so will the behavior" (1959:241). For White as for Kroeber, culture was an au-

---

*In 1975, Leslie White modified his thinking somewhat, bringing it more in line with Kroeber's: "We no longer think of culture as designed to serve the needs of man; culture goes on its own way in accordance with laws of its own" (1975:159).

tonomous realm, to be conceived of as totally independent not only of heredity in general, but also of human mentality or consciousness in particular. While Kroeber may not have been interested in human behavior as such, he, no less than White, saw it as a "dependent variable" relative to culture. Both believed culture theory could progress only by holding the human being constant, by ignoring the concrete human being of our experience and, for purposes of anthropological analysis, assuming human mentality to be nothing more than the product of culture.*

It is therefore not surprising that both Kroeber and White argued at length against the so-called "great man" theory of history. In "The Superorganic," Kroeber declares:

> When we cease to look upon invention or discovery as some mysterious inherent faculty of individual minds which are randomly dropped in space and time by fate; when we center our attention on the plainer relation of one such advancing step to the others; when, in short, interest shifts from individually biographic elements—which can only be dramatically artistic; didactically moralizing, or psychologically interpretable—and attaches wholeheartedly to the social or civilizational, evidence on this point will be infinite in quantity, and the presence of majestic forces or sequences pervading civilization will be irresistibly evident. (1917:45)

Here White's dismissal of human creativity in the distinction between symbol and sign (1944) is matched by Kroeber's distinction between the individual and "majestic forces or sequences." To this latter statement Edward Sapir replied in 1917:

> All individuals tend to impress themselves on their social environment and though generally to an infinitesimal degree, to make their individuality count on the direction taken by the never-ceasing flux that the form and content of social activity are inevitably subject to . . . Shrewdly enough Dr. Kroeber chose his examples from the realm of inventions and scientific theories. Here it is easy to justify a sweeping social determinism in view of a certain general inevitability in the course of the acquirement of knowledge. (1917:441–42)

---

*Kroeber did not find White's concept of "culturology" basically foreign to his own thought: "In these statements I do not feel that I am, as White thinks, failing to 'hold consistently to the culturological point of view,' I am only delimiting and trying to clarify it" (1952:115).

From this response through the remainder of his career, we can trace a logical course of development in the thought of Sapir that displays an increasingly conscious realization that the concepts of "society" and "individual" are to be meditated by the concept of "culture"—by bringing culture down to the empirically rich level of the concrete experiencing human being of our own private lives.

In 1924 Sapir was to write:

> There is no real opposition, at last analysis, between the concept of a culture of the group and the concept of an individual culture. The two are interdependent . . . An automatic perpetuation of standardized values, not subject to the constant remodeling of individuals willing to put some part of themselves into the forms they receive from their predecessors, leads to the dominance of impersonal formulas. The individual is left out in the cold; the culture becomes a manner rather than a way of life, it ceases to be genuine. It is just as true, however, that the individual is helpless without a cultural heritage to work on. (1924:417–18)

In 1927 he wrote that "all human behavior involves essentially the same types of mental functioning, as well conscious as unconscious, and that the term 'social' is no more exclusive of the concept 'unconscious' than is the term 'individual' for the very simple reason that the terms 'social' and 'individual' are contrastive in only a limited sense" (1927:544). In 1928 he was to observe: "What constitutes spiritual serenity must be answered afresh for every culture and for every community, in the last analysis, for every individual" (1928:346). In 1935 he observed:

> The interests connected by the terms culture and personality are necessary for intelligent and helpful growth because each is based on a distinctive kind of imaginative participation by the observer in the life around him. The observer may dramatize such behavior as he takes note of in terms of a set of values, a conscience which is beyond self and to which he must conform, actually or imaginatively, if he is to preserve his place in the world of authority or impersonal social necessity. Or, on the other hand, he may feel the behavior as self-expressive, as defining the reality of individual consciousness against the mass of environing social determinants . . . One is as subjective or objective as the other, for both are essentially modes of projection of personal experience into the analysis of social phenomena. (1934:591)

In 1938 he declared that "problems of social science differ from problems of individual behavior in degree of specificity, not in kind" (1938:573). Finally, in 1939 he stated:

> No formulations about man and his place in society which do not prove strictly and literally accurate when tested by the experience of the individual can have more than a transitory or technical authority. Hence we need never fear to modify, prune, extend, redefine, rearrange, and reorient our sciences of man as social being, for these sciences cannot point to an order of nature that has meaning apart from the directly experienced perceptions and values of the individual. (1939:581)

While Kroeber devoted the remainder of his career to the study of culture as the historical investigation of impersonal forces manifest in sequences of cultural patterns, Sapir developed his sense of anthropology as history into an increasingly vital commitment to the study of the history of the individual. By seeing human creativity not in terms of "a purely individual contribution" but as "a blending of form to one's will" (1924:321), and by seeing meaningful existence not simply as a matter of indoctrination and mindless conformity, but as putting some part of oneself into the received symbolic forms, Sapir took the concept of culture to the level of the human being of our experience. Thus Sapir and Benedict both made fundamental contributions to anthropology by attempting to synthesize it with personality theory. Kroeber, like many anthropologists after him, largely ignored this fundamental challenge to impersonal culture theory, viewing it as a "subfield" of anthropology peripheral to the dominant concerns of cultural anthropology, rather than as a fundamental rethinking of our disciplinary concept (see Toulmin 1972). Kroeber never understood the theoretical import of Sapir's "Do We Need a Superorganic?" His misunderstanding was perpetuated as the largely unexamined misunderstanding so prevalent in American anthropology to this day, of the so-called subfield of "culture and personality." To both Sapir and Benedict it was not enough to consider the individual in terms of culture; one had to consider culture in terms of the individual as well. Thus they helped to establish contemporary humanistic anthropology in general and scientific humanism in particular.

In 1947 we find Kroeber observing:

> Culture-and-personality may be construed essentially as an attempted use of culture to understand personality better. It is interested in people and their behavior, less in forms of culture. It is legitimate as a shift of focus and problem, not as a new attack on old problems. Culture consideration enters into its purview only peripherally, as a means. If culture remains the distinctive core subject matter of anthropology, culture-and-personality must be regarded as a marginal province thereof. (1947:108).

This was a fundamental misreading of the Sapirian project.

Kroeber and Kluckhohn, in their discussion of various definitions and conceptualizations of "Culture and Psychology," note that "it is highly convenient to construct an abstract conceptual model of a culture. But this does not mean that culture is a force like Newtonian gravity 'acting at a distance.' Culture is a precipitate of history but, as internalized in concrete organisms, very much active in the present" (1952:222). It was Kroeber's assumption that culture was a simple determinant of human behavior that justifies the impersonal conceptualization of culture. It was precisely the appreciation of the variation and complexity involved in how cultural forms are "internalized in concrete organisms" that motivated Sapir's 1917 reply to Kroeber. Sapir was not using "culture to understand personality better," but personality to understand culture better. By looking in minute detail at the actual human acquisition of culture, by looking at the actual human experience from which culture was abstracted, we could come to a more mature understanding of the concept of culture itself.

In his anthropological thinking, Sapir was attempting a "new attack on old problems." He was creating a research strategy that viewed forms of culture as historically bequeathed human creations with which other human beings in turn willfully and creatively attempted to make sense of their lives, their human experiences, through the extremely complex interaction of received forms, reflective awareness, and willful initiative. Human existence, cultural existence, required personal interpretation, personal sensemaking. As Sapir was to observe in 1934:

> The complete, impersonalized "culture" of the anthropologist can really be little more than an assembly or mass of loosely overlapping idea and action systems which, through verbal habit, can be made to assume the appearance of a closed system of behavior. What tends to be forgotten

is that the functioning of such a system, if it can be said to have any ascertainable function at all, is due to the specific functioning and interplays of the idea and action systems which have actually grown up in the minds of given individuals . . . It may be proper for the systematic ethnologist to ignore. . . . pattern differences. . . . but for the theoretical anthropologist, who wishes to place culture in a general view of human behavior, such an oversight is inexcusable. (1934:594, 596)

Sapir's developing culture theory was an attempt to conceptualize culture in terms of the species-specific characteristics that simultaneously united and differentiated human beings rather than in terms of an analogy to physical forces of nature. To realize this aim, he saw the locus of culture in human consciousness rather than in an abstraction of such consciousness called "society." Such a conceptualization of culture is of great significance for a historical understanding of the development of humanistic anthropology, symbolic anthropology, and such recent areas of interest as narrative anthropology. However, it may be in the development of anthropological approaches to Western and other modern societies that the Sapirian perspective is most sorely needed.

Kroeber's inability fully to appreciate the fundamental theoretical challenge posed by Sapir's "Do We Need a Superorganic?" has been mirrored in the indifference of succeeding generations of cultural anthropologists to Sapir's theoretical writings. It is not surprising, therefore, to hear Kroeber state in 1950 that "an approach manageable by anthropologists which will yeild an adequate functional interpretation or even formulation of a living large civilization as a totality still remains to be worked out" (1950:150). This is as true in 1989 as it was in 1950. The reason, then as now, is the impersonal conceptualization of culture.

As long as we fail to focus on human consciousness as the locus of culture, we will continue to have great difficulty in applying anthropology to our own society. When we think of culture impersonally and see it as a force rather than as a medium, we are led to the dogma that culture must be shared, and we survey heterogeneous modernity with dismay (see White 1959:244, 246). This dogma bears the historical traces of the concept of culture's development out of the concept of custom. We need to stop seeing the customary as the shared, and see it rather as the bequeathed, forms of and for human sensemaking, creativity, and freedom. When we do so, we can come to understand the freedom in restraint, the classical spirit, that Sapir tried to locate in cultural anthropology by seeing it in the common cultural nature of all humanity. Such a vision of humanity, while recognizing the existential isolation of all human minds (an isolation exacerbated by contemporary heterogeneity), is not a psychiatric reading of the human condition. It is a natural moral reading of the cultural condition as being as applicable to anthropologists as it is to those they study. It is a vision that transmutes isolation into personalism. As a scientific humanist, Sapir sought the moral implications of anthropological fact in his classic essay, "Culture, Genuine and Spurious." He states in the opening of the essay, "I propose to give my idea of what kind of a good thing culture is" (1924:308). To his mind, the distinction between "is" and "ought" implied choice rather than disillusionment, as he came to see cultural existence as a personal process of making sense. By focusing on culture in terms of concrete human experience—by understanding it as adaptation not only to the physical world but also to the mental world, the human consciousness that presents that physical world to us—Sapir came to appreciate the uniqueness and complexity that is the meaningful existence of each individual. Culture can be shared only when we look from the outside, in general terms, at the cultural other. As Sapir noted in 1924, "the genuine culture is internal, it works from the individual to ends" (1924:316). This is as true for the scientific humanist within anthropology as it is for the normal individual outside of anthropology. While Sapir did not realize the full implications of what he was saying in 1917, nevertheless he observed of anthropology: "Historical science thus differs from natural science, either wholly or as regards relative emphasis, in its adherence to the real world of phenomena, not, like the latter, to the simplified and abstract world of ideal concepts. It strives to value the unique or individual, not the universal" (1917:446).

By 1934 Sapir was prepared to state, apropos of the anthropology of modern society:

> The cultures so carefully described in our ethnological and sociological monographs are not, and cannot be, the truly objective entities they claim to be. No matter how accurate their individual itemization, their integrations into suggested structures are uniformly fallacious and unreal. This

cannot be helped so long as we confine ourselves to the procedures recognized as sound by orthodox ethnology. If we make the test of inputting the contents of an ethnological monograph to a known individual in the community which it describes, we would be inevitably led to discover that, while every single statement in it may, in the favorable case, be recognized as holding true in some sense, the complex of patterns as described cannot, without considerable absurdity, be interpreted as a significant configuration of experience, both actual and potential in the life of the person appealed to. Cultures, as ordinarily dealt with, are merely abstracted configurations of idea and action patterns, which have endlessly different meanings for the various individuals in the group. (1934:593)

Anthony Wallace has noted that all we must ask of the concept of culture in relation to the concept of society is that these individual totalities or mazeways have sufficient areas of equivalence for behavioral coordination—i.e., for society—to transpire (1970).

Sapir realized that human experience, meaningful existence, genuine cultural being, is far too complex to continue the impersonal charade. To bring the anthropological record to bear on modern life, we must seek "totality" in the experience of the concrete human being, beginning with ourselves trying to communicate something personal to whatever audience there may be.

In 1952 Kroeber confessed, "We seem not yet to have attained a concise, unambiguous, inclusive and exclusive definition of culture" (1952:23). But it is also true that Sapir "never gave a full-length formal definition of culture" (Kroeber and Kluckhohn 1952:273). While I shall not attempt to put forward that which Sapir alone could have formulated, I believe that the essence of a Sapirian concept of culture is present in his writings. It is culture as symbolically mediated experience, human experience considered from the perspective of meaningfulness. By symbolically mediated experience I mean, for example, that we decide whether to describe abortion as murder or not, and in that descriptive decision, we decide whether or not it *is* murder. Starting from an initial interest in linguistics, Sapir came to see culture in terms of human consciousness, and human consciousness in terms of symbolics, forms personally made meaningful. He believed that the study of humanly satisfying or genuine culture involved the investigation of the symbolics of natural moral (or valued) existence in its psychosocial unity. His sophistication was matched by the complexity of the data he chose to investigate.

Sapir realized that, when we take culture to the level of the individual, when we look at life history as culture, we come to appreciate cultural forms as vehicles for meaningful (i.e., valued) human existence. It is ironic that, by ignoring Sapir, by the consistent trivialization of his cultural writings, anthropology has made itself an example of culture seen as the symbolic mediation of experience. Sapir has been a victim of the contemporary Western division of human understanding into "psychology" as distinct from "anthropology" and "sociology." There is, however, no logical reason, only a culturological one, for this division. As Sapir realized, the study of culture is the most powerful naturalistic approach to contemprary human behavior and experience precisely as it seeks to synthesize "psychology" and "sociology," the "individual" and "society," in terms of a culture-talk that speaks directly to the consciousness and spirit of its audience.

To recapture the mature Sapirian perspective is to return with renewed understanding to the serious consideration of Freud's significance for anthropology. Kardiner and Preble observe of Freud:

> His first attempt to account for some aspects of man's social life (in *Totem and Taboo*) was completely rejected by anthropologists, and justifiably so. He had gone to the literature of evolutionary anthropology for confirmation of his psychological theory of human development. Specifically, he was looking for evidence that the experiences of primitive man were constitutional determinants in the life of modern man. This Lamarckian bias of Freud and most of his followers, and the devastating criticism of evolutionary anthropology by Boas, Goldenweiser, and Kroeber, disqualified the use of Freudian ideas in anthropology. (1961:12, 13)

But Freud was not looking simply for a historical confirmation that could only be conjectural and thus rightly criticized, but rather for a congruence between his reading of human consciousness and human society. As with Sapir, it was the search for this congruence that informed his understanding of culture.

Kardiner and Preble go on to observe that "social institutions and social change are incomprehensible without a knowledge of human ontogenetic development, human motivation and the inner workings of the mind" (1961:13). However, Freud, like Sapir, never provided a formal definition of culture that exemplified his personal conceptualization in terms of human consciousness. He went little further than to speak of civilization or culture as "all those respects in which human life has raised itself above its animal status and differs from the life of beasts" (1927, 21:5–6).

While Sapir came to a personal conceptualization of culture by starting with the social, Freud came to it by starting with the individual. In the postscript which he added in 1935 to his "Autobiographical Study," he states: "My interest, after making a long detour through the natural sciences, medicine, and psychotherapy, returned to the cultural problems which had fascinated me long before, when I was a youth" (1959, 20:72). I believe that Freud's mature sense of culture, like that of Sapir, can be fruitfully understood in terms of the symbolic mediation of experience, with particular emphasis on values or "the superego," as Freud would have it. Freud, like Sapir, was a scientific humanist, and his approach to human consciousness and thus to culture was, if it was anything, symbolic.

The whole of Freud's metapsychology is an attempt to constitute understanding by putting symbol to personal experience. His interests in jokes, verbal slips, language as entry point to consciousness, dreams, art, and literature speaks to his symbolic orientation. His concepts of "displacement," "projection," and "sublimation," for example, all depend on the human symbolizing ability. Indeed, his very constitution of human consciousness in terms of "clinical inference" (Geertz 1973a:26) speaks to his symbolic or interpretive approach to human reality.

To both Sapir and Freud, human symbolic consciousness, our awareness of being aware through forms of meaning, was the key to understanding culture. Not surprisingly, both came to see the needs of human consciousness, and thus of culture, primarily in terms of self-acceptance, self-control, and existential affirmation. I believe it is fair to say that Sapir would see an existence in which awareness was not integrated with caring as a spurious cultural or human existence, and Freud would see it as illness. They both developed humanistic approaches to culture, based on the logical analysis of human experience and the personal consequences of cultural existence. Their writings on culture were progressively converted into naturalistic moral discourses, discussions of "is" in relation to "ought," addressed to the common humanity of their audiences. Their mature writings were meditations on the relationship between human suffering and morality, on the consequences for human being of human consciousness as manifest in cultural existence. While Sapir tended to emphasize the positive or optimistic possibilities, Freud tended to emphasize the negative or pessimistic realities. But both approached the ideal through the real. By 1924 Sapir was talking of genuine culture in terms of human values, and Freud's interest in human maturity had led by the mid-1920s to a focus on culture in terms of the superego. He stated in the concluding pages of *Civilization and Its Discontents*:

> I believe that the line of thought which seeks to trace in the phenomena of cultural development the part played by a super-ego promises still further discoveries. I hasten to come to a close. But there is one question which I can hardly evade. If the development of civilization has such a far reaching similarity to the development of the individual and if it employs the same methods, may we not be justified in reaching the diagnosis that under the influences of cultural urges, some civilizations, or some epochs of civilization—possibly the whole of mankind—have become "neurotic"? (1930, 21:144)

In Sapir's 1928 essay, "The Meaning of Religion," we see his growing realization that culture as the symbolic mediation of experience is capable of a humanization, and in this sense a therapeutic transcendence, of material reality. Moreover, it is this transcendence that is at the heart of genuine culture, the adaptation of human consciousness to itself. He talks with a personal voice of an individual's feeling of community with a necessary universe of values (1928:356). He says of religion: "it aims at nothing more nor less than the impulsive conquest of reality" (1928:348).

Freud's discussions of religion, while searching for the human truths of culture, could not, for personal reasons, get beyond seeing religion in terms of human need. Thus Freud simply focused on the relationship between need and belief, on religion as illusion, as Geertz was to do some thirty-seven years later (Geertz 1964). But while Freud could not come to a mature view of culture through his studies of religion, he did come to see the essence of genuine culture in his essay on humor written in 1927.

In *Jokes and Their Relation to the Unconscious*, written in 1905,

Freud considered humor strictly from a scientific perspective. He saw humor in terms of his postulated psychic energies of human consciousness, his so-called "economic point of view." He saw humor in terms of pleasure produced by an economy of expenditure in feeling. It was, to his mind, like wit and the comic, a temporary return to a childhood in which we were not engaged in the serious psychic work of adulthood. He had yet to develop his topological division of the mind into id, ego, and superego. It was, I believe, his acute interest in the latter, the superego, that stimulated his renewed interest in culture in general and specifically caused him to return to a consideration of humor. In his 1927 essay "Humor," we can detect the beginnings of a transformed sense of human existence as symbolically mediated or cultural existence, a Sapirian sense.

In that essay, Freud, after alluding to his earlier work, asks, "What are the dynamics of the adoption of the humorous attitude?" His example of this attitude is the following: "A criminal who was being led out to the gallows on a Monday remarked: 'Well, the week's beginning nicely'" (Std. Ed. 21:162). Freud answers his own question by asserting that "we obtain a dynamic explanation of the humorous attitude . . . if we assume that it consists in the humorist's having withdrawn the psychological accent from his ego and having transposed it to his super-ego" (Std. Ed. 21:164). Earlier in the essay, Freud had identified the superego with "the parental agency," the presenter of received value forms to the child. While Freud had difficulty seeing the superego in a favorable light in relation to either religion or his therapeutic work, he caught a glimpse of its heroic, transcendent dimension, of culture as a symbolic stance toward life, in his mature analysis of humor. Thus we find Freud speaking of humor in terms of "grandeur," "elevation," and "dignity," rather than simply in terms of pleasure, as he had done in 1905.

Sapir could see in the religious attitude "the pursuit, conscious or unconscious, of ultimate serenity following total and necessary defeat" (1928:347). Through symbolic mediations that called forth moral or valued being, genuine culture, in the guise of the religious attitude, appeared to Sapir as "the triumph of human consciousness" (1928:347). Typical of Sapir's mature view of culture, he notes: "What constitutes spiritual serenity must be answered afresh for every culture and for every community—in the last analysis, for every individual" (1928:347).

Freud came to the truth of genuine culture as symbolic mediation through his return to a contemplation of the humorous attitude. He attained a realization he was repeatedly denied in his several returns to a contemplation of the religious attitude. He wrote in 1927:

> In what, then, does the humorous attitude consist, an attitude by means of which a person refuses to suffer, emphasizes the invincibility of his ego in the real world, victoriously maintains the pleasure principle—and all this, in contrast to other methods having the same purposes, without overstepping the bounds of mental health (21:163).

His answer is the dominance of the superego, which is now seen in a new light. Thus, he states in the final paragraph of his essay, "If it is really the super-ego which, in humor, speaks such kindly words of comfort to the intimidated ego, this will teach us that we still have a great deal to learn about the nature of the super-ego" (21:166).

It is not surprising that Sapir and Freud should have arrived at their deepest appreciations of culture as symbolic mediation of experience through the contemplation of the religious and humorous attitudes respectively, for both attitudes are genuine humanizations of reality, aspects of the transcendent moral potentiality of the spirit of human consciousness as symbolic consciousness. As Konrad Lorenz observed in "Avowal of Optimism," the closing chapter of *On Aggression*:

> G.K. Chesterton has voiced the altogether novel opinion that the religion of the future will be based to a considerable extent on a more highly developed and differentiated, subtle form of humor. Though, in this formulation, the idea may appear somewhat exaggerated, I feel inclined to agree, answering one paradox with another by saying that we do not as yet take humor seriously enough. (1967:293)

It is my faith that by understanding cultural existence as symbolically mediated experience, we can, perhaps, take a more conscious, restrained, and thus spiritually mature responsibility for reading humanity into the natural world.

I shall end in the spirit of scientific humanism by quoting from Woody Allen's "Hasidic Tales, with a Guide to Their Interpretation by the Noted Scholar":

Rabbi Zwi Chaim Yisroel, an Orthodox scholar of the Torah and a man who developed whining to an art unheard of in the West, was unanimously hailed as the wisest man of the Renaissance by his fellow-Hebrews, who totalled a sixteenth of one percent of the population. Once, while he was on his way to synagogue to celebrate the sacred Jewish holiday commemorating God's reneging on every promise, a woman stopped him and asked the following question: "Rabbi, why are we not allowed to eat pork?" "We're not?" the Rabbi said incredulously. "Uh-oh." (1978:51)*

---

*From *Getting Even* by Woody Allen, copyright © 1971. Reprinted by permission of Random House, Inc.

REFERENCES

Aberle, David F.
1960   The Influence of Linguistics on Early Culture and Personality
       Theory. In *Essays in the Science of Culture*, ed. Gertrude E. Dole
       and Robert L. Carniero, p. 1–29. New York: Crowell.
Agassi, Joseph, and Ian Jarvie
1967   "The Problem of the Rationality of Magic." *British Journal of An-
       thropology* 18:55–74.
Allen, Woody
1978   *Getting Even*. New York: Vintage Books.
Beals, Ralph
1978   Sonoran Fantasy or Coming of Age? *American Anthropologist* 80:
       355–62.
Bellah, Robert
1970   *Beyond Belief: Essays on Religion in a Post-Traditional World.*
       New York: Harper and Row.
Benedict, Ruth
1923   The Concept of the Guardian Spirit in North America. *Memoirs
       of the American Anthropological Association* 29:1–97.
1959   *Patterns of Culture*. Boston: Houghton Mifflin. Orig. ed. 1934.
1946   *The Chrysanthemum and the Sword: Patterns of Japanese Culture.*
       Boston: Houghton Mifflin.
Berryman, John
1976   The Development of Anne Frank. In Berryman, *The Freedom of the
       Poet*, 91–106. New York: Farrar, Straus, and Giroux.
Beth, Loren
1958   *The American Theory of Church and State*. Gainesville: Univer-
       sity of Florida Press.
Boas, Franz
1928   *Anthropology and Modern Life*. Revised edition, 1932. New
       York: Norton.

130 Humanistic Anthropology

1969a   Intellectual Freedom. In Boas, *Race and Democratic Society*, pp.
        175–77. New York: Biblo and Tannen.
1969b   Role of the Scientist in Democratic Society. In Boas, *Race and
        Democratic Society*, pp. 215–19. New York: Biblo and Tannen.
Bowen, Elinore Smith
1964   *Return to Laughter*. Garden City, N.J.: Doubleday.
Bronowski, Jacob
1973   *The Ascent of Man*. Boston: Little, Brown.
1977   *A Sense of the Future*. Cambridge: MIT Press.
Bunzel, Ruth
1968   Edward Sapir. In *The Golden Age of American Anthropology*, ed.
        Margaret Mead and Ruth L. Bunzel, pp. 439–40. New York:
        George Braziller.
Cassirer, Ernst
1946   *The Myth of the State*. New Haven: Yale University Press.
Castaneda, Carlos
1968   *The Teachings of Don Juan: A Yaqui Way of Knowledge*. New
        York: Ballantine Books
1971   *A Separate Reality: Further Conversations with Don Juan*. New
        York: Simon and Schuster.
1972   *Journey to Ixtlan: The Lessons of Don Juan*. New York: Simon
        and Schuster.
1973   Sorcery: A Description of the World. Ph.D. diss., UCLA.
Chuangtse
1963   Chuangtse Dreaming of Being a Butterfly. In *The Wisdom of Lao
        Tzu*, ed. Lin Yutang, p. 238. New York: Modern Library.
Dawidowicz, Lucy
1977   Jewish Identity: A Matter of Fate, a Matter of Choice. In Dawid-
        owicz, *The Jewish Presence*, pp. 3–31. New York: Holt, Rinehart
        and Winston.
De Mille, Richard
1976   *Castaneda's Journey: The Power and the Allegory*. Capra Press.
1980   *The Don Juan Papers: Further Castaneda Controversies*. Santa
        Barbara, Calif.: Capra Press.
Diamond, Stanley
1974   *In Search of the Primitive: A Critique of Civilization*. New Bruns-
        wick, N.J.: Transaction Books.
Dostoevsky, Fyodor
1929   *The Brothers Karamozov*. New York: The Modern Library.

Durkheim, Emile
1915   *The Elementary Forms of the Religious Life.* Glencoe, Ill.: Free Press.
1933   *The Division of Labor in Society.* Glencoe, Ill.: Free Press. Orig. ed. 1893.
1973   Individualism and the Intellectuals. In *Emile Durkheim on Morality and Society*, ed. Robert N. Bellah, pp. 43–57. Chicago: University of Chicago Press.
Eisley, Loren
1946   *The Immense Journey.* New York: Random House.
Eliade, Mircea
1971   *The Myth of the Eternal Return.* Princeton, N.J.: Princeton University Press.
Evans-Pritchard, Edward
1952   Religion and the Anthropologists. In *Social Anthropology and Other Essays*, pp. 158–71. New York: Free Press.
1962   *Social Anthropology and Other Essays.* New York: Free Press.
1965   *Theories of Primitive Religion.* New York: Clarendon.
Falwell, Jerry
1980   *Listen America!* Garden City, N.J.: Doubleday.
Firth, Raymond
1957   Malinowski as Scientist and as Man. In *Man and Culture*, ed. Raymond Firth, pp. 1–14. New York: Harper.
Frazer, James
1910   *Totemism and Exogamy.* 4 vols. London: Macmillan.
1918   *Folklore in the Old Testament.* 3 vols. London: Macmillan.
1933   *The Fear of the Dead in Primitive Religion.* London: Biblo and Tannen.
1951   *The Golden Bough.* 3rd ed. 12 vols. London: Macmillan.
Freud, Sigmund.
1905   *Jokes and Their Relation to the Unconscious.* London: Hogarth Press.
1925   *An Autobiographical Study.* Standard Edition, 20:7–70. London: Hogarth Press, 1959.
1927   The Future of an Illusion. Standard Edition, 21:3–56. London: Hogarth Press, 1961.
1927   Humour. Standard Edition, 21:159–66. London: Hogarth Press 1961.
1930   *Civilization and Its Discontents.* Standard Edition, 21:61–145. London: Hogarth Press, 1961.
1935   Postscript. Standard Edition, 20:71–74. London: Hogarth Press, 1959.
Gay, Peter
1978   *The Enlightment: An Interpretation.* Vol. 2. New York: Knopf.

Geertz, Clifford
1973a   Thick Description: Toward an Interpretive Theory of Culture. In
         Geertz, *The Interpretation of Cultures*, pp. 3–30. New York: Basic
         Books.
1973b   Deep Play: Notes on the Balinese Cockfight. In Geertz, *The Inter-
         pretation of Cultures*, pp. 412–53. New York: Basic Books.
1973c   Religion as a Cultural System. In Geertz, *The Interpretation
         of Cultures*, pp. 87–125. New York: Basic Books. Originally
         published in *Anthropological Approaches to the Study of Re-
         ligion*, ed. Michael Banton, pp. 1–46. London: Tavistock,
         1966.
1975   Common Sense as a Cultural System. *Antioch Review* 33:5–26.
1976   Art as a Cultural System. *Modern Language Notes* 91:1473–99.
1983   Found in Translation: On the Social History of the Moral Imagin-
         ation. In Geertz, *Local Knowledge: Further Essays in Interpretive
         Anthropology*. New York: Basic Books.
Gerth, Hans, and C. Wright Mills
1958   *From Max Weber: "Essays in Sociology."* New York: Galaxy
         Books.
Goodmen, Mary Ellen
1967   *The Individual and Culture*. Homewood, Ill.: Dorsey.
Grice, H. Paul
1971   Meaning. In *Readings in the Philosophy of Language*, ed. J.F. Ros-
         enberg and C. Travis. Englewood Cliffs, N.J.: Prentice-Hall.
Hallowell, A. Irving
1967   *Culture and Experience*. New York: Schocken.
Hamilton, A., J. Madison, and J. Jay.
1847   *The Federalist*. Philadephia: Desilver. Originally published by J.
         and A. McClean, 1788.
Harris, Marvin
1968   *The Rise of Anthropological Theory*. New York: Thomas Y.
         Crowell.
Harner, Michael J.
1967   Jívaro Souls. In *Gods and Rituals: Readings in Religious Beliefs
         and Practices*, ed. John Middleton, pp. 177–95. Garden City, N.J.:
         Natural History Press.
Hays, Hoffman
1964   *From Ape to Angel*. New York: Capricorn.
Henry, Jules
1963   *Culture Against Man*. New York: Random House.

Herskovits, Melville
1955   Cultural Relativism and Cultural Values. In Herskovits, *Cultural Anthropology*. New York: Knopf.
Honigmann, John
1976   The Personal Approach in Cultural Anthropological Research. *Current Anthropology* 17:243–61.
Hsu, Francis
1971   Psychosocial Homeostatis and Jen: Conceptual Tools for Advancing Psychological Anthropology. *American Anthropologist* 73:23–44.
Kaberry, Phyliss
1957   Malinowski's Contribution to Field-work Methods and the Writing of Ethnography. In *Man and Culture*, ed. R. Firth, pp. 71–92. New York: Harper.
Kardiner, Abram, and Edward Preble
1961   *They Studied Man*. New York: Mentor.
Kroeber, Alfred
1917   The Superorganic. In Kroeber, *The Nature of Culture*, pp. 22–51. Chicago: University of Chicago Press, 1952.
1935   Review of *Patterns of Culture*. *American Anthropologist* 37:689–90.
1947   Causes in Culture. In Kroeber, *The Nature of Culture*, pp. 107–109. Chicago: University of Chicago Press, 1952.
1948   White's View of Culture. In Kroeber, *The Nature of Culture*, pp. 110–17. Chicago: University of Chicago Press, 1952.
1950   The History and Present Orientation of Cultural Anthropology. In Kroeber, *The Nature of Culture*, pp. 144–51. Chicago: University of Chicago Press, 1952.
1952   *The Nature of Culture*. Chicago: University of Chicago Press.
1963   *Style and Civilizations*. Berkeley: University of California Press.
Kroeber, Alfred, and Clyde Kluckhohn
1952   *Culture: A Critical Review of Concepts and Definitions*. New York: Vintage Books.
Langer, Susanne
1957   *Philosophy in a New Key: A Study In the Symbolism of Reason, Rite and Art*. Cambridge, Mass.: Harvard University Press.
Langness, Lewis, and Gelya Frank
1978   Fact, Fiction and the Ethnographic Novel. *Anthropology and Humanism Quarterly* 3:18–22.
Lao Tzu
1963   *Tao Te Ching*. Translated by D.C. Lau. Baltimore: Penguin.

Leach, Edmund
1957   The Epistemological Background to Malinowski's Empiricism. In *Man and Culture*, ed. R. Firth, pp. 119–38. New York: Harper.
Leavis, F.R.
1963   *Two Cultures? The Significance of C.P. Snow and an Essay by Michael Yudkin*. New York: Pantheon.
Lee, Dorothy
1949   Being and value in a primitive culture. *Journal of Philosophy* 46(13):401–415.
1950   Codifications of reality: lineal and nonlineal. *Psychosomatic Medicine*, 12(5):89–97.
Lessa, William, and Evon Vogt, editors
1965   *Reader in Comparative Religion: An Anthropological Approach*. New York: Harper and Row.
Lorenz, Konrad
1963   *On Aggression*. New York: Harcourt Brace Jovanovich. Reprinted, Bantam Books, 1967.
Malefijt, Annemarie de Waal
1968   *Religion and Culture*. New York: Macmillan.
Malinowski, Bronislaw
1913   *The Family Among the Australian Aborigines*. New York: Schocken. Rpt. ed. 1963.
1922   *Argonauts of the Western Pacific*. New York: Dutton. Rpt. ed. 1952.
1926   *Crime and Custom in Savage Society.*. London: Routledge and Kegan Paul.
1927   *Sex and Repression in Savage Society*. New York: Humanities Press.
1929   *The Sexual Life of Savages in Northwestern Melanesia*. New York: Harcourt, Brace and World.
1935   *Coral Gardens and Their Magic*. Reprint ed. Bloomington: Indiana University Press, 1965.
1944a   *Freedom and Civilization*. Reprint ed. Bloomington: Indiana University Press, 1960.
1944b   *A Scientific Theory of Culture*. Chapel Hill: University of North Carolina Press.
1948   *Magic, Science and Religion and Other Essays*. Garden City, N.Y.: Anchor Books. Originally published by the Free Press, 1948.
Mandelbaum, David
1973   The Study of Life History: Gandhi. *Current Anthropology* 14:177–206.

Mead, Margaret
1959a *An Anthropologist at Work: The Writings of Ruth Benedict.*
       Boston: Houghton Mifflin.
1959b A New Preface. In Ruth Benedict, *Patterns of Culture*, pp. vil–x.
       Boston: Houghton Mifflin.
1974   *Ruth Benedict.* New York: Columbia University Press.
Nadel, Siegfried
1953   Social Control and Self-Regulation. *Social Forces* 31:265–73.
1957   Malinowski on Magic and Religion. In *Man and Culture*, ed. R.
       Firth. pp. 189–208. New York: Harper.
Needham, James, ed.
1925   *Science, Religion and Reality.* New York: Macmillan.
Ong, Walter
1969   World as view and world as event. *American Anthropologist*
       71:634–47.
Pelto, Pertti, and Gretel Pelto
1975   Intra-Cultural Diversity: Some Theoretical Issues. *American
       Ethnologist* 2:1–18.
Pfeffer, Leo
1953   *Church, State, and Freedom.* Boston: Beacon Press.
Polanyi, Karl
1944   *The Great Transformation.* New York: Rinehart.
Rasmussen, Knud
1930   *Intellectual Culture of the Hudson Bay Eskimos.* Copenhagen:
       Gyidendaiski Boghandel, Nordisk Fortag.
Redfield, Robert
1953   *The Primitive World and Its Transformation.* Ithaca, N.Y.: Cornell
       University Press
Reps, Paul
1959   *Zen Flesh, Zen Bones.* Translated by P. Reps. Ruthland: C.E.
       Tuttle.
Rice, Kenneth
1980   *Geertz and Culture.* Ann Arbor: University of Michigan Press.
Richardson, Miles
1975   *Anthropologist—The Myth Teller.* American Ethnologist 2:517–33.
Rieff, Philip
1963   *Culture and Character.* New York: Collier Books
1966   *The Triumph of the Therapeutic: Uses of Faith after Freud.* New
       York: Harper and Row.
1972   *Fellow Teachers.* New York: Harper and Row.

1979   *Freud: The Mind of the Moralist.* Third edition. Chicago: University of Chicago Press.

Robinson, Ian.

1976   Shamanism. In *Encyclopedia of Anthropology,* eds. David E. Hunter and Phillip Witten, p. 350. New York: Harper and Row

Roszak, Theodore

1969   *The Making of a Counter Culture.* Garden City, N.Y.: Doubleday.

Rubenstein, Richard L.

1966   *After Auschwitz: Radical Theology and Contemporary Judaism.* New York: Bobbs-Merrill.

Sahlens, M.

1968   *Tribesman.* Englewood Cliffs, N.J.: Prentice Hall.

Sapir, E.

1917   Do We Need a Superorganic? *American Anthropologist:* 19:441–47.

1924   Culture, Genuine and Spurious. In *Selected Writings of Edward Sapir,* ed. David G. Mandelbaum, pp. 308–31. Berkeley: University of California Press, 1949.

1927   The Unconscious Patterning of Behavior in Society. In *Selected Writings of Edward Sapir,* ed. David G. Mandelbaum, pp. 544–59. Berkeley: University of California Press, 1949.

1928   The Meaning of Religion. In *Selected Writings of Edward Sapir,* ed. David G. Mandelbaum, pp. 346–56. Berkeley: University of California Press, 1949.

1934   The Emergence of the Concept of Personality in a Study of Cultures. In *Selected Writings of Edward Sapir,* ed. David G. Mandelbaum, pp. 590–97. Berkeley: University of California Press, 1949.

1938   Why Cultural Anthropology Needs the Psychiatrist. In *Selected Writings of Edward Sapir,* ed. David G. Mandelbaum, pp. 569–77. Berkeley: University of California Press, 1949.

1939   Psychiatric and Cultural Pitfalls in the Business of Getting a Living. In *Selected Writings of Edward Sapir,* ed. David G. Mandelbaum, pp. 578–89. Berkeley: University of California Press, 1949.

1949   *Language: An Introduction to the Study of Speech.* New York: Harcourt, Brace and World First edition, 1921.

1963a   The Meaning of Religion. In *Selected Writings of Edward Sapir,* ed. David G. Mandelbaum, pp. 346–56. Berkeley: University of California Press, 1949.

1963b   The Emergence of the Concept of Personality in a Study of

Cultures. In *Selected Writings of Edward Sapir*, ed. David G. Mandelbaum, pp. 590–97. Berkeley: University of California Press, 1949. In *Selected Writings of Edward Sapir*, ed. David Mandelbaum, pp. 590–97. Berkeley: University of California Press, 1949

Schmidt, Paul
1955   Some Criticisms of Cultural Relativism. *Journal of Philosophy* 52:780–91.

Schneider, David: Janet Dolgin; and David Kemnitzer
1977   As People Express Their Lives, So They Are. In *Symbolic Anthropology: A Reader in the Study of Symbols and Meanings*, ed. David M. Schneider, Janet L. Dolgin, and David S. Kemnitzer, pp. 3–44. New York: Columbia University Press.

Scholte, Bob
1969   Toward a Reflexive and Critical Anthropology. In *Reinventing Anthropology*, ed. Dell Hymes, pp. 430–57. New York: Random House.

Shankman, Paul
1984   The Thick and the Thin: On the Interpretive Theoretical Program of Clifford Geertz. *Current Anthropology* 25:261–79.

Shelley, Percy
1965   A Defence of Poetry. In *Defence of Poetry: The Four Ages of Poetry*: ed. John E. Jordan, pp. 25–80. New York: Bobbs-Merrill. Orig. ed. 1839.

Singer, Isaac Bashevis, and Ira Moskowitz
1976   *A Little Boy in Search of God: Mysticism in a Personal Light*. Garden City, N.J.: Doubleday.

Snow, C.P.
1961   *The Two Cultures*. New York: Cambridge University Press.

Szasz, Thomas
1976   *Heresies*. Garden City, N.J.: Doubleday.

Toulmin, Stephen
1972   *Human Understanding*. Princeton, N.J.: Princeton University Press.

Turnbull, Colin
1962   *The Forest People*. Garden City, N.J.: Doubleday.

Tylor, Edward
1865   *Researches into the Early History of Mankind and the Development of Civilization*. Rpt. ed. Chicago: University of Chicago Press, 1964.
1871   *Primitive Culture*. Rpt. ed. New York: Harper, 1958.
1899   *Anthropology: An Introduction to the Study of Man and Civilization*. New York: D. Appleton. First edition, 1881.

Wagner, Roy
1975   *The Invention of Culture.* Englewood Cliffs, N.J.: Prentice-Hall.
Wallace, Anthony
1956   Revitalization Movements. *American Anthropologist* 58:264–81.
1970   *Culture and Personality.* 2d ed. New York: Random House.
Wax, Murray, and Rosalie Wax
1963   The notion of magic. *Current Anthropology* 4:495–518.
White, Leslie
1944   The Symbol: The Origin and Basis of Human Behavior. *Etc: A Review of General Semantics* 1:229–37.
1959   The Concept of Culture. *American Anthropologist* 61:227–51.
1975   *The Concept of Cultural Systems: A Key to Understanding Tribes and Nations.* New York: Columbia University Press.
Wilk, Stan
1972   Review of Carlos Castaneda, A Separate Reality. *American Anthropologist* 74:921–22.
1976   Cultural Materialism and Cultural Idealism. *Anthropology and Humanism Quarterly* 1:9–11.
1977   Castaneda: Coming of Age in Sonora. *American Anthropologist* 79:84–91.
1980   Don Juan on Balance. In *The Don Juan Papers,* ed. R. DeMille. Santa Barbara, Calif.: Ross-Erikson.
Winch, Peter
1964   Understanding a Primitive Society. *American Philosophical Quarterly* 1 307–324.
Witt, Elder, ed.
1980   *The Supreme Court and Individual Rights.* Washington, D.C.: Congressional Quarterly.
Wittgenstein, Ludwig
1967   Remarks on Frazer's "The Golden Bough." *Synthese* 17:233–53.
Wolf, Eric
1964   *Anthropology.* Englewood Cliffs, N.J.: Prentice Hall.
Wordsworth, William
1940   *The Poetical Works of William Wordsworth.* Edited by E. de Selincourt, New York: Oxford University Press.

INDEX

Aberle, David, 87
abortion, 97, 106, 121
absolutist enculturation, 31, 107. *See also* cultural absolutism
aesthetic naturalism, xii, 31
affect: anthropology and, 60–61, 63; Ruth Benedict and, 19, 29, 31, 32; citizenship and, 94, 99, 105, 106; cultural relativism and, 20, 26, 27–28, 31; faith and, 40; intellect and, 26; magic and, 54–55; needs, 63, 102; religion and, 56, 63; science and, 63; understanding and, 22–23, 60–61, 62. *See also* ethos.
affirmation, 20, 25, 80, 82, 83, 87, 89
Agassi, Joseph, 23
alienation, 22, 25, 29, 89
Allen, Woody, 126–27
American Anthropological Association, 37, 39
animism, 48–49
anomie, 89
anthropology: affect and, 24, 60–61; as art, 22–23, 25, 28, 68, 69, 73; awareness and, 17, 78; as caring inquiry, 23; creation science and, 39; as the cultivation of common humanity, 24–25, 39; cultural other and, 43, 57, 66, 69; democracy and, 93–107 passim; description and, 23, 24, 69, 73; experience and, 78; as history, 117; as human creativity, 23–24, 28, 36; human ecosystem and, 23; humanities and, 57; interpretation and, 67–77 passim;

legitimacy of, 96; life of the mind and, 71; love and, 23, 26, 31, 36; meaning and, 74, 78, 92; as a metacultural system, 39; as a moral discipline, 24–25, 28, 36, 39, 78; as moral science, 89; myth and, 3, 4, 24, 63, 73, 92; patterns of culture and, 24; personal professional distinction in, 20, 22, 35–40 passim, 78; psychology and, 122; as a science fiction, 70; humanism in, 24, 35–40 passim; sociology and, 122; as a spiritual discipline, 28; suffering and, 31–33; teaching of, 23, 34, 36–40 passim, 80, 91–92; values and, 22, 38, 45; as a way of life, 20, 24, 25, 28, 39
appreciative identification, 24, 62, 66
art, 23, 25, 28, 29, 31, 64, 69, 73, 85
art of living, 14, 25, 28, 63, 89. *See also* personal artistry
Auschwitz, 2, 77

Bambuti, 6, 75
Bellah, Robert, 64
Benedict, Ruth: affect and, 19, 29, 31, 32; alienation and, 22, 25; biography of, 22, 32–33; concept of social maturation, 24; cultural absolutism and, 28, 33–34, 38; cultural relativism and, 26, 27–28, 29, 30–31; culture-consciousness and, 11, 20, 21, 31–32; emotional maturity and, 23, 26, 33; empathy, 23, 27–28; faith, 33–34; Jerry

Benedict, Ruth (*continued*)
Falwell and, 26; concept of integration, 16; Kwakiutl, 90; modern mind and, 26, 29; perspective on anthropology, 23–26, 111–12; poetry, 19, 28, 31, 34; principal of cultural relativism, 31; psychosocial, 26, 29, 30, 31, 32, 33, 112, 117; Pueblos, 30; self-creation, 24, 26, 29, 38; sense of difference, 22; teaching of anthropology, 23; value discourse, 25; well being, 17, 29
Berryman, John, 80
Boas, Franz, 44, 93, 94, 95, 106, 107
Bohannon, Laura [pseud. Elinore Smith Bowen], 12
Bowen, Elinore Smith [pseud. Laura Bohannon]
Bronowski, Jacob, 37–38, 63, 77
Buddha, 67
Bunzel, Ruth, 85–86
Burger, Warren, 101

caring, 22, 27, 123
Cassirer, Ernst, 5
Castaneda, Carlos, xi, 11, 82, 83, 84, 88, 91. *See also* Don Juan
change, 75, 104
character, 81, 86, 91
Cheyenne, 75
choice, 75, 76, 77, 98, 120. *See also* morality
Christ, 40, 77
Chuangtse, 2. *See also* Lao Tzu
church and state, 93–107 passim
classical spirit, 177
common humanity: anthropological understanding and, 22, 24, 26, 29, 35, 39, 62; contemporary society and, 88; cultural relativism and, 20, 24, 26, 62; faith and, 34; forgiveness and, 28; humanism and, 24–25; as moral being, 24, 30, 31–32, 39; Sapir and, 80–81;

therapeutic anthropology and, 89; as the unity of empathy and self-knowledge, 24, 28–29, 62–63; Wittgenstein and, 61. *See also* morality
communism, 99–100
comparative method, 24, 26, 45, 61
conformity, 11, 14, 21, 105–6, 117
creation science, xi, 37, 39, 60, 62
creativity: Ruth Benedict and, 11, 21, 22–23, 24, 29, 30, 38, 111–12; collective tradition and, 78, 83, 84, 119–20; cultural anthropology and, 28, 44–45, 68, 74, 78; culture process and, 22, 78, 82–83; equality and, 31; Clifford Geertz and, 7, 73, 82–83; history and, 21; interpretation and, 74, 76; judgment and, 62, 75; love and, 36; moral imagination and, 21, 36, 62, 75, 76; needs and, 21, 78; as personal, 7, 21, 22, 75, 78, 83, 84, 119–20; in relation to society, 111–14; responsibility and, 11, 75–76; the sacred and, 75–76; Edward Sapir and, 83, 84; science and, 68–69, 75–76; scientific humanism and, 76; supernatural beliefs and, 60, 62, 75–76; symbolics and, 4, 5, 7, 14–15, 78, 83; Leslie White and, 115
Cromwell, Oliver, 77
cults, 100
cultural absolutism, 26, 27, 28, 38, 40. *See also* absolutist enculturation
Cultural animal, 22, 78
cultural idealism, 45
cultural immersion, 27
cultural other, 17, 26, 27, 29, 32, 45, 57, 61, 62. *See also* self
cultural pluralism, 26, 91, 107, 120
cultural realities: anthropology as, 3, 40; Ruth Benedict and, 23, 65; as constitutive of human life worlds, 3, 23, 65; cultural resources and, 65; definition of, 6; Don Juan and,

82; human consciousness and, 7; human creativity and, 9, 84; the individual and, 65, 84, 89; self-exploration and, 84; as stances toward life, 23, 65. *See also* culture
cultural relativism: appreciative identification and, 62; the beautiful and, 40; Ruth Benedict and, 26, 27–28, 29, 30–31; Franz Boas and, 94–95; change and, 33–34; emotional maturity and, 26, 27–28; ethnocentrism and, 27, 30–31; explanation and, 62–63; faith and, 34, 62; genius and, 22; human emotions and, 20, 26, 27–28, 30–31; as humanism, 25–26, 33–34; Melville Herskivits and, 26–27, 29, 69, 94–95; interpretive description and, 22–23; love and, 26, 27–28, 30–31; as natural moral doctrine, 25, 29, 30–31, 33–34; orthodoxy and, 33–34; personal sensemaking and, 29; personalism and, 24, 62; psychosocial and, 21, 29, 30, 33; science and, 33–34, 77; scientific humanism and, 24, 25; self-knowledge and, 29, 62; as social ethic, 29, 33–34, 94–95; synthesis of method and motivation, 26; understanding and, 26, 28, 29, 61, 62–63; universal logic and, 20, 28; will to love and, 26, 27–28, 77; world history and, 69. *See also* natural moral discourse
cultural universals, 86
culture: anthropology and, 4, 44–45, 78; art and, 21, 27–28, 73; Ruth Benedict's concept of, 26; Franz Boas and 44–45; creativity and, 21, 22, 23, 27–28, 89; dogma and, 71; Sigmund Freud's definition of, 122–23; Clifford Geertz's perspective on, 67–77 passim; human consciousness and, 16, 45, 78, 119–20, 123, 124; Clyde Kluckhohn and

Alfred Kroeber's definition of, 45; as a making, 26, 65, 89; Bronislaw Malinowski's concept of, 54; meaning and, 78, 87, 89; moral science and, 89; needs and, 10, 15, 16, 54, 78, 123; Edward Sapir's perspective on, 78–92 passim, 111–27 passim, 122–23; as a science of fiction, 69–70; as a stance toward life, 57, 65; symbolics and, 7, 15, 65, 78; Roy Wagner's concept of, 68; as a way of life, ix, 23, 28; Leslie White's perspective on, 15, 114–15; Stan Wilk's definition of, 78. *See also* culture-consciousness
culture-consciousness: Ruth Benedict and, 11, 20, 21, 31–32; common humanity and, 20, 31–32; creativity and, 23, 32; cultural realities and, 23; defined, ix, 8, 24; disharmony and, 16; Emile Durkheim and, 83; eternal return and, 12, 13; human experience and, 23, 40; identity and, 31; judgment and, 11, 27; maturity and, 23; models and, 8, 87; modern society and, 87; morality and, 10, 23, 31–32; mystery and, 13–14, 17; participant observation and, 40; personal change and, 23; self-knowledge and, 21, 23, 40; tolerance and, 17; value description and, 22–23, 25, 32. *See also* culture
culture and experience, 5, 15–16, 21, 23, 78, 85, 88, 118, 120–21
culture and the individual, 16, 21, 65, 84–86, 89, 114–15, 119–21. *See also* culture and personality, personal sensemaking, personality
culture and personality, 15, 85, 116, 118. *See also* personality
culture process, 12, 14, 16, 22, 24, 84. *See also* human consciousness, human experience
culture theory: as appropriate descrip-

culture theory (*continued*)
    tion, 22–23, 78; impersonal,
    112–13, 114–16, 117, 121; inter-
    pretive, 67–77 passim; Alfred
    Kroeber and, 82, 112–13, 114–16,
    117; as myth making, 12, 16–17,
    72, 73, 91–92; as personal
    sensemaking, 40; prediction and,
    72; scientific humanism and, 24,
    38; subjectivity and, 61–62; Leslie
    White and, 6, 15–16, 82, 114–16
customary mind, 27, 30, 62. *See also*
    culture-consciousness
cybernetics, 15

Dawidowicz, Lucy S., 91
death, 22, 26, 33, 48, 125
defensiveness, 27. *See also*
    ethnocentrism
description, 4, 21, 22, 24, 25, 29–30,
    31, 69, 73, 84, 118–19, 120–21. *See
    also* translation, value description
Diamond, Stanley, 34, 86–87
difference, 17, 19, 27, 28, 31, 32, 34,
    37, 43, 45, 61, 75, 92, 122
dignity, 26
discovery, 12, 24–25, 37, 84, 91–92, 115
disharmony, 6–7, 16, 29, 89, 116, 123.
    See also alienation
dogma, 71, 77, 93
Don Juan, xi, 17, 79, 80, 82, 83, 84,
    86, 89, 90, 91, 92
Dostoevsky, Fyodor, 40
Durkheim, Emile: Geertz and, 67,
    69–70: on mechanical solidarity,
    87; on modern society, 86; on
    moral science, 76, 89; on religion,
    67, 75–76; religious background,
    46; on sacred, 75–76; on self-
    restraint, 99

Eisley, Loren, 8–9, 10
emotional certainty, 26. *See also*
    cutlural absolutism
emotional needs, 63, 102. *See also*

human motivation, human nature,
    human needs
emotionalism, 95
empathic understanding, 22, 25, 27,
    28–29, 30, 32, 60, 62. *See also*
    humanistic anthropology
empathy: caring and, 27;
    characteristics of, 62; choice and,
    31; common humanity and, 24;
    comparative method and, 24, 27;
    experience and, 62; facts and, 20;
    identification and, 62; isolation
    and, 62; Bronislaw Malinowski
    and, 62; self and, 96; self-
    knowledge and, 24, 27, 28–29;
    Ludwig Wittgenstein and, 60, 62;
    wonder and, 17–18. *See also*
    humanistic anthropology
enculturation, 31, 58, 85
enlightenment, 93, 95, 96, 99, 103, 104
eternal return, 16. *See also* wisdom
ethnocentrism: absolutism and, 27, 31,
    87; among anthropologists, 46, 59,
    64, 87; art and, 28; Ruth Benedict
    and, 29–30; customary mind and,
    30–31; defensiveness and, 27; Don
    Juan and, 89; fear and, 27;
    Bronislaw Malinowski and, 59;
    tolerance and, 27. *See also* cultural
    absolutism
ethos, 22–23, 25. *See also* affect
Evans-Pritchard, Edward, 11, 46–47,
    70–71, 74–75, 91
evolutionism, 45
existential mystery, ix, 4, 14, 17, 35, 65,
    81. *See also* human experience
experiential irresolvability, 86
explanation, 61, 62

faith: anthropology and, 40, 58,
    76–77; Ruth Benedict and, 33–34;
    common humanity and, 64;
    cultural relativism and, 33–34, 62;
    defined, 7; Galileo and, 38;
    humanistic anthropology and, ix,

39, 40, 58, 61; inquiry and, 39, 58, 76–77; meaning and, 74; myth and, 7; natural reason and, 94; necessity and, 19; personal sensemaking and, ix; progress and, 45, 59; reason and, 64; religion and, 76–77; science and, 76–77; scientific humanism and, ix, 34, 39, 61, 64; self and, ix; supernatural and, 50, 76–77; symbolics and, 126; truth and, 39, 40, 76–77. *See also* personal sensemaking; self

Falwell, Jerry, 26, 39, 64, 96, 97, 98, 99–100, 103, 104, 105

fear, 17, 27, 28

fieldwork, 52

Firth, Raymond, 53

forgiveness, 28–29

Frazer, James, 43, 46, 47, 50–51, 57–58, 59, 60, 62

freedom, 33, 74, 82, 93–107 passim, 119–20. *See also* creativity

Freud, Sigmund, viii, xii, 46, 63, 122–26 passim

Galileo, 37–38

Gay, Peter, 96, 104

Geertz, Clifford, 8, 67–77 passim, 123; on common sense, 8; interpretive theory, 64, 72–74; on models, 7, 8, 68; Edward Sapir and, 81, 82–83; on symbolic anthropology, 84; the therapeutic and, 10, 83

genuine culture: existential challenge and, 77, 83; the individual and, 78, 81, 121–22; integrity and, 86; as living tradition, 27; moral imagination and, 21; Edward Sapir's concept of, 78, 81, 83–84, 87, 116, 121–22, 123–24; in scientific humanism, 63; the spurious and, 123; the state and, 100; transcendence and, 125; values and, 124

Goethe, 91

Goldenweiser, Alexander, 122

Goodmen, Mary Ellen, 16

Grice, Paul, 68

Haddon, A.C., 51

Hallowell, A. Irving, 4, 8

happiness, 100–101. *See also* maturity

Harris, Marvin, 44–45

Helms, Jessie, 103

Henry, Jules, 9–10, 15, 16

heroism, 22, 31, 77, 125

Herskovits, Melville, 26, 29, 69, 94, 95

history: Ruth Benedict and, 21, 34, 111–12; Sigmund Freud and, 122, 124; Melville Herskovits and, 69; Alfred Kroeber and, 111, 112, 115, 117; Heinrich Rickert and, 72; Edward Sapir and, 72–73, 81, 111, 117, 118, 120, 122; the United States and, 93, 102, 103, 104; Leslie White and, 115

Hitler, Adolph, 35, 36, 40

holistic orientation, 8, 16

Hsu, Francis, 15, 16

human behavior, 14, 21, 118–19, 120–21

human biology, 21, 44, 112–13

human consciousness: awareness and, 7, 8, 10, 11, 12, 14–15, 78, 123; cross-cultural studies and, 61; culture and, 16, 45, 78, 119–20, 123, 124; disharmony and, 11, 14–16; Loren Eisley and, 10; experience and, 7, 14–15, 78: Sigmund Freud and, 122, 123–24; Clifford Geertz and, 7, 67, 70, 73, 75: the good life and, 6–7, 11, 12, 14–15, 17–18, 61; human life and, 10, 14–15, 22–23, 73, 78, 82, 119; isolation and, 10, 61, 62; mystery and, 2, 4, 14, 65, 67, 103; religion and, 107; Edward Sapir and, 81, 84, 85, 118–19, 123–24; science and, 6, 7, 61, 63, 65, 70, 73, 77, 93; scientific humanism and, 39; social

human consciousness (*continued*)
life and, 15–16, 22, 33, 34, 65, 89,
122; subjectivity and, 7, 61–62, 65,
78: symbolics and, 7, 14–15, 78,
82–83, 91–92, 123; Ludwig Wittgenstein and, 61
human experience: culture and, 13;
ethos and, 22; meaning and, 78;
mystery and, 14, 75; as process, 8;
realization in, 17; religion and, 75,
76; sacrilization and, 77; universals
and, 89. *See also* existential mystery
human motivation: anthropology and,
22, 25, 26, 78; Ruth Benedict and,
22, 25–26; culture and, 78, as
spirit, 25–26, 32. *See also* emotional needs, meaning
human nature, 5, 7, 11, 21, 32, 78, 86,
88. *See also* emotional needs
human needs, 16, 21, 29, 63, 64, 78,
85, 120, 123. *See also* emotional
needs, symbolic needs
human spirit, 19, 25, 26, 32, 33, 62, 64
humanism, ix, 21–22, 24–25, 28, 30,
39, 64, 88
humanistic anthropology: common
humanity and, 24, 32, 123–24; the
cultural other and, 62; cultural
relativism and, 27; description and,
62; Don Juan and, 84; Sigmund
Freud and, 123–24; natural moral
being and, ix; natural moral
discourse and, 28; patterns of
culture and, 21, 25; personal
sensemaking and, ix; reinterpretation and, 91; Edward Sapir and,
85, 88, 123–24; the teaching of,
38–39. *See also* humanism
humanities, 37, 57, 61
humor, viii, 124–25, 126–27

identifying with others, 20, 22, 62. *See
also* empathy
identity, 25, 31, 90–91. *See also* personal sensemaking, self

ideologies, 28
illusion, 16, 47, 60–61, 84
imagination, 21, 73
individual, the, 28, 65, 78, 80, 84–85,
115, 120. *See also* culture and the
individual
inquiry, 39, 61, 62
integrity, 38, 39, 86, 91
intellectualism, 45, 47, 59
interpretation: Ruth Benedict and,
22–23, 29–30; cultural relativism
and, 22–23, 29–30; description
and, 4, 22–23, 29–30; Sigmund
Freud and, 123; Clifford Geertz
and, 67–77 passim; meaning and,
74; personal sensemaking and, 38;
Edward Sapir and, 116–21 passim;
theory and, 67–77 passim; values
and, 22. *See also* description
invention, 115
is/ought, 27, 39, 63, 95, 120, 123. *See
also* natural moral discourse
isolation, 2, 3, 61, 120. *See also*
alienation

Jarvie, Ian, 23
Jefferson, Thomas, 102–3
Jewish, being, x, 19, 35, 46, 75, 90–91,
126–27
Jivaro, 17
Jones, Bob III, 103
judgment, 27, 29, 62, 81. *See also*
ethnocentrism

Kluckhohn, Clyde, 45, 118
Kroeber, Alfred, 11, 45, 81, 82, 85,
112–22 passim
Kwakiutl, 90

language, 78, 85, 86, 87
Lao Tzu, 65, 67, 81, 85. *See also*
Chuangtse
Leach, E.R., 58
Leavis, F.R., 37
Lee, Dorothy, 59

legality, 102
legitimacy, 71, 96, 101, 102
Levy-Bruhl, Lucien, 46, 54
life history, 122
literature, 37, 79
logic, 13, 20, 22, 27, 28. *See also* logicoempirical
logicoempirical, 22, 96, 97–98, 103. *See also* logic
Lorenz, Konrad, 32, 126
love, ix, x, 20–21, 22, 24, 26, 27–28, 30, 31, 36, 92

Madison, James, 94, 104, 105
magic, 68–119 passim
Malefijt, Annemarie de Waal, 47, 57
Malinowski, Bronislaw, 43, 46, 51–62
materialism, 9
maturity: Ruth Benedict and, 23, 24, 27; contemporary, 23, 73; the cultural other and, 66, 70; culture-consciousness and, 23, 24, 69; Don Juan books and, 82; emotional, 26, 27, 66; Jerry Falwell and, 26; Sigmund Freud and, 124; myth and, 73–74; naivete and, 61; reading in and, 126; scientific humanism and, 39, 61; self and, 27; spirituality and, 126
Mead, Margaret, 7–8, 44, 111
meaning, 15, 68–69, 72, 74, 78, 80
Mensch, 63
metaculture, 13, 39, 74
method, 8, 22, 26
Montague, Ashley, 44–45
moral issues, 25, 27, 95
moral majority, 96
moral order, 60, 64, 76, 87
morality: affect and, 22, 27, 32, 61; anthropology and, 25, 29, 36, 38–39, 112; beauty and, 31–32; creativity and, 21, 119–20; cultural relativism and, 25–26, 29; Sigmund Freud and, 123–24, 125; imagination and, 21, 32, 62; legality and, 102;

motivation and, 26, 40, 44; poetry and, 19–20; reading in, ix; Robert Redfield and, 11, 40; Edward Sapir and 21, 81, 119–20, 123–24; scientific humanism and, ix, 36, 38, 64; self and, 22, 27, 29, 32, 61, 62–63; society and, 77; suffering and, 35, 123–25; subjectivity and, 61; transcendence and, 126; truth and, 39, 64, 77; Stan Wilk and, 35. *See also* value
description
Morgan, Lewis Henry, 44
myth: anthropology and, 3; Ruth Benedict and, 24; Ernst Cassirer and, 5; definition of modern myth, 4, 7; Eskimo, 13–14; Clifford Geertz and, 73–74; meaning and, 73–74; of opposition, 16–17: Edward Sapir and, 81; scientific humanism and, 76
mythic movement, 4, 63, 70, 72, 73–74, 76. *See also* meaning

Nadel, Siegfried, 14, 15
narrative anthropology, 119. *See also* Castaneda, Carlos
natural moral being, ix, 29, 35–40, 63, 65. *See also* naturalism
natural moral discourse, 27, 28, 29, 38, 39, 60, 63, 81, 95, 123. *See also* cultural relativism
natural rights, 99
naturalism, 23, 28, 38, 62, 93–107 passim. *See also* logicoempirical
naturalistic reasoning, 32, 96, 103, 106–7
neoshamanism, ix
Nietzsche, 30
nihilism, 33
nonrational, 43, 94
normality, 11, 22, 31

objectivity, 20, 61, 69, 83, 116. *See also* science

partiality, 16
participant observation, 23–24, 40, 52
Pelto, Gretel, 87
Pelto, Pertti, 87
personal artistry, 21, 28, 29, 84, 85, 89.
    See also art of living
personal sensemaking, ix, 22, 29, 39,
    100, 118, 120
personality, 85, 116, 118–19. *See also*
    character, culture and the in-
    dividual, culture and personality
philosophical anthropology, 38
Plato, 36
poetry: Ruth Benedict and, 19, 28, 31,
    34; empathy and, 28, magic and,
    60–61; religion and, 60–61;
    Richard Rubenstein and, 2;
    shamanism and, 89; Percy Shelly
    and, 19; supernatural beliefs and,
    60, 62; technology and, 82;
    William Wordsworth and, 34
politicians, 104
postmodern, the, 84, 86, 87, 88, 91
power, 39, 77
preaching, 39
primitive, 12, 16, 34, 66, 86–87
privacy, 95, 98, 100
progress, 45, 59
psychology, 113, 122
psychosocial: common humanity and,
    24; comparative method and, 24,
    25, 29; as cultural being, 111–12;
    cultural relativism and, 21, 26, 31;
    empathic understanding and, 31;
    homeostasis, 16; interpretation and,
    29; love and, 31; morality and, 24,
    121–22; scientific technology and,
    38; self-development and, 26, 29;
    values and, 22, 25, 121–22
psychosocial homeostasis, 16
pueblos, 30

Rasmussen, Knud, 13
rational ideals, 95
reading in, ix, 76, 126

Reagan, Ronald, 103
Redfield, Robert, 11, 16, 40, 87
refinement, 80–81
reflexive anthropology, 3
reinterpretation, 91. *See also* personal
    sensemaking
religion: absolutism and, 65; affect
    and, 56; experience and, 76–77:
    Sigmund Freud and, 124; Clifford
    Gertz and, 67–77 passim, 76–77;
    illusions and, 124; magic and, 43–65
    passim; origins of, 47, 79; other
    cultures and, 46, 75; poetry and,
    60–62; primitive, 46–47, 70–71,
    78–79; Edward Sapir and, 124,
    125–26; science and, 38, 39, 43–77
    passim, 63–64, 65, 73–75; super-
    natural and, 64; understanding and,
    75. *See also* supernatural beliefs
religious Right, xi, 39, 64, 96, 99, 100,
    105. *See also* Falwell, Jerry
respect, 26, 77
responsibility, 8, 11, 17–18, 92, 126
revitalization movement, 15
Richardson, Miles, 3, 92
Rickert, Heinrich, 72
Rieff, Philip, 10, 11–12, 22, 36, 63, 71,
    89
right to life, 97, 106
Roszak, Theodore, 8
Rubenstein, Richard, 2

Sahlins, Marshall, 66
Sapir, Edward, xi, xii; Carlos
    Castaneda and, 79–90, 88; concep-
    tualization of culture, 88; on
    creativity, 84; Don Juan and,
    79–80, 89; historical science and,
    72, 111, 115, 122; the individual
    and, 78–92 passim, 111–27 passim;
    language metaphor and, 87; per-
    sonal meaning and, 80; on
    psychosocial, 116, 120–21, 122;
    spurious culture, 16, 123; on taste,
    80; on teaching, 80

Schmidt, Wilhelm, 47
Scholte, Bob, 3
science: anthropology and, 37, 38, 69; fiction of, 70, 73; forgiveness and, 28–29; freedom and, 38, 140; the habitual and, 106–7; historical, 72–73; human needs and, 63; humility and, 77; interpretive, 67–77 passim; magic and, 50–51, 56, 57, 58, 60, 61, 62, 63; Bronislaw Malinowski and, viii, 59, 61; moral, ix, 13, 76; myth and, 73; natural, 13, 73; religion and, 38, 39, 43–77 passim, 63–64, 65, 73–74; scientific humanism and, ix, 24, 36, 38; subjectivity and, 63, 65, 69
scientific humanism: affect and, 63, 76; anthropology and, 24, 35–40 passim, 62; art and, 23; caring inquiry and, 23, 76; certainty and, 77; common humanity and, 64; cultural relativism and, 24, 25; existential mystery and, 65; faith and, ix, 34, 39, 61, 64; hermeneutics and, 39; as metaculture, 39–40; morality and, ix, 36, 38, 64, 76; science and, ix, 24, 36, 38; supernatural beliefs and, 39, 63; values and, 64
scientism, 45, 61
secular humanism, xi, 39
self: anthropology and, 38, 62–63; common humanity and, 62; conflict and, 17; as conscious moral being in the making, 22; culture and, 21; expressiveness and, 116; humanistic anthropology and, ix; mystery and, ix, 4, 14, 81; personal sensemaking and, ix; shamanism and, 17; sociality and, 89; tradition and, 27, 84; tolerance and, 17–18
self-awareness, 2, 4, 8, 9, 27, 62
self-development, 22, 26, 29, 124
self-exploration, 39, 62, 84

self-knowledge, viii, 21, 24–25, 27, 28–29, 61–62
self-restraint, 94, 95, 99
self-righteousness, 27
Seligman, C.G., 51
Shakespeare, William, 19
shamanic warrior, 17, 83, 91
shamanism, 13, 16, 17, 32, 77, 78–79, 83–84, 89, 92
Singer, Isaac Bashevis, 35, 39
Snow, C.P., 37
social sciences, 57, 61, 69, 96, 117
sociality, 15, 31, 32, 52, 65, 89
society, 65
society, modern, 86–89
sociology, 122
Socrates, 29, 100
Spencer, Herbert, 44
stories, 3, 9–10, 13. *See also* myth
Story, Joseph, 93
subjectivity, 2, 20, 61–62, 63, 65, 116
sublimation, 60
suffering, 9–10, 31, 33, 35, 124, 126
superego, 124, 125, 126
supernatural beliefs, 39, 43–77 passim, 57, 61–62, 63–64, 76–77, 84. *See also* religion
superorganic, 81, 111
Swaggart, Jimmy, 64
symbol, 3, 6, 19–20, 14–16, 60, 78, 82, 115, 123
symbolic anthropology, 8, 14–16, 78, 82, 83, 84, 119
symbolic needs, 15–16, 78. *See also* human needs
Szasz, Thomas, 12–13

teaching anthropology, 34, 35–40, 80–81, 91–92
technology, ix, 60
temperament, 21
theology, 2, 71, 77
therapeutic anthropology, 4–5, 8, 9, 10, 11, 13, 14, 15–17, 39, 74, 80, 83, 89, 123

tolerance: anthropology and, 26, 77; Ruth Benedict and, 17–18, 33–34; cultural relativism and, 17–18, 26–27, 33–34, 63; freedom of choice and, 98; Clifford Geertz and, 77; Melville Herskovits and, 26–27, 94–95; human diversity and, 94–95; humility and, 77; public issues and, 27, 94; of self and other, 17–18: self-knowledge and, 63

totalitarianism, 99, 100, 101

tradition, 2, 11, 20, 21, 27, 45, 78, 83, 104

transcendence, 9, 16, 82, 124–26

translation, 62, 69, 91

Trobriand Islanders, 52, 54, 57, 59

trust, 17

truth, 13, 22, 25, 36, 38, 39, 40, 63, 64, 69, 70, 92, 102

Tylor, Edward Burnett, 43, 44, 46, 44–50, 53, 55–56, 57, 59, 60

understanding: affect and, 22–23, 60; appreciation and, 26, 60, 61, 62–63, 82–83; cultural relativism and, 26, 28, 29, 61, 62–63; Eskimo mythology and, 13–14; Bronislaw Malinowski and, 60; mystery and, 13–14, 75; personalism and, 62–63; religion and, 75; shamanism and, 13–14; the symbolic and, 78, 82–83; Ludwig Wittgenstein and, 60. *See also* empathic understanding

utilitarianism, 45, 59, 87

value description, 22–23, 25, 32, 116

values: affect and, 22, 33, 95; anthropology and, 22, 33–34, 81, 87; behavior and, 14, 87, 116; Ruth Benedict and, 17, 22, 30, 32, 38; cultural relativism and, 33–34, 38, 94; culture and, 45; description and, 22, 25; empathy and, 32; genuine culture and, 124; human creativity and, 22; inquiry and, 33, 116; interpretation and, 22; judgment and, 81; motivation and, 22; Siegfried Nadel and, 14, 15; political, 102; psychosocial and, 22; rational ideals and, 95; Edward Sapir and, 81, 116, 124; science and, 38, 63–64; teaching anthropology and, 38. *See also* value description

vision, 16, 20

Wagner, Roy, 23, 68

Wallace, Anthony, 15, 73, 87, 121

Weber, Max, 37

wellbeing, 8, 14, 17, 25, 39, 74, 78, 87, 89, 100–1

White, Leslie, 6, 15, 82, 113, 114–15

Wilk, Stan, 4, 73, 89

will, 21, 26, 72

wisdom, viii, 13, 14, 63, 67, 81. *See also* eternal return

Wittgenstein, Ludwig, 93–97, 102

Wolf, Eric, 43

Wordsworth, William, 34

world view, 38, 39, 40, 63